Jeffrey W. Hanna

Safe and Secure

The Alban Guide to Protecting Your Congregation

An Alban Institute Publication

Library of Congress Card Number 99-72201

ISBN 1-56699-211-7

CONTENTS

96477

FOREWORD

"What are your securities?"

In *Safe and Secure*, Jeff Hanna shows how security is more a church question than a Merrill-Lynch question.

Of course, security *is* big business. Personal security is even bigger business. In 1997 $62 billion was spent on private security, a figure that most likely will double in the next couple of years. The private security market is predicted to grow at 8.5 percent a year through 2002.[1] In cuisine, security or comfort foods—meatloaf, mashed potatoes, stews—have made a huge comeback. In colleges, security issues are given top priority in everything, from dorms to software to grading.

To understand security issues in our time, however, we must look beyond the practical issues to consider the theological, historical, and cultural contexts that inform them. We must consider three things in particular: our condition, our culture, and our call. First is our condition: sin. This is a world where people neither behave nor believe according to the purpose for which they were created. We are "dead in our trespasses and sins" (Ephesians 2:1). The historical tenure of original sin has been documented in innumerable ways. For instance, in John Keegan's Reith Lectures on "War and Our World," the eminent historian argues and substantiates that the 20th century has witnessed humanity at its cruelest and most horrific: 10 million dead in World War I, 50 million killed in World War II, and over 50 million killed in conflicts since.[2] The riveting, disturbing war images in Steven Spielberg's 1998 movie *Saving Private Ryan* bring those statistics to horrible life. Or, if that is not enough to convince you, pick up any daily newspaper detailing violence against children perpetrated by their parents or caretakers. In the face of such overwhelming evidence, it is difficult to maintain a "people-are-basically-good" romanticism.

The apostle Paul was not the first to discover that "there is no one righteous, not even one" and that "all have sinned and fall short of the glory of God" (Rom 3:10, 23). Or as my mother used to say, "Boys, you aren't sinners because you sin. You sin because you're sinners." Failure to come to grips with the magnitude of evil lurking in each one of us is failure to grasp the biblical truth that we are only as good as our last worst act.

In this theological sense, therefore, all security is an illusion. Nothing is secure. Nobody is secure. Only freedom brings security. The more freedom we have to make choices and pursue our own interests, the more secure we become. The more freedom we experience in Christ, the greater our securities. Our only real security is eternal security.

Second, our culture is in TEOTWAWKI transition. TEOTWAWKI stands for The End Of The World As We Know It. It's not simply that the 500-year reign of the modern world is over and a postmodern world is being born. The establishment of the Christian church in Western culture ("Christendom") is dead. What is more, Christianity itself is dying in the West. The world that was, was Christian-friendly. Post-modern culture is at best indifferent, at worst hostile, to Christianity.

The litigiousness of this emerging culture knows no bounds. As Hanna shows, inadequate security will leave churches vulnerable to skulking lawsuits as well as the spread of new crimes like computer hacking, hate crimes, terrorism, and so forth. The number of terrorist incidents in the world, many of which were directed against houses of worship, increased more than 300 percent in the last three decades.[3]

A smart ministry mandates securities. The church must hope for the best while anticipating worse-case scenarios. The church's role of stockpiling food and pharmaceuticals that could be used by communities in cases of emergency is an example of a "smart" ministry.

Third, our calling is to be in mission where God is at work. God is as much at work in the world as in the church (some would argue more so). Unfortunately, in the risk-averse world of the church, we play it safe with our mission—and play fast and loose with our inheritance.

As I write these words, an evening news report features the theft from a Seattle church of toys collected for homeless children. "Who would do such a thing?" is the reporter's refrain. No one, however, asked the questions Hanna proposes in this book: Why would a church leave itself so insecure that such a theft was possible?

God is doing a new thing in our congregations and our wider community. We can take risks out there because we take care in here.

Take risks, church. But first, take care.

Leonard Sweet
Dean of the Theological School
Vice President of Drew University

ACKNOWLEDGMENTS

I wish to offer my thanks to the following:

Almighty and Loving God, for leading me along paths that finally answered the question of how my past in law enforcement and current ministry could come together.

My wife, Karla, and sons, Kurt and Kyle, for enduring many frequent, wild ideas and for encouraging me to follow through and complete one. Ta-Da!

My parents, for giving me the foundation of faith I needed to get where I am today.

The victims and victors of congregational-related crimes who shared their stories and insights.

The congregations that I have had the privilege of serving.

Those who acted as advisors: George Cochran, Tim Friend, Fred Lawman, Rusty Taylor, Scott Figgens, Bob Aldridge, and Thomas Taylor.

The Alban Institute staff, especially my acquisitions editor, Beth Ann Gaede.

INTRODUCTION

Behold, I send you out as sheep in the midst of wolves; therefore be shrewd as serpents, and innocent as doves (Matt. 10:16, NAS).

In one sense it saddens me to write this book. It seems unbelievable that the family of God has come to a time when churches and congregations have to be concerned with security and safety.

We think of congregations as places of rest, safety, and nourishment for souls. We are shocked when we hear that a pastor's, leader's, or teacher's conduct has been called into question. We are amazed when we read that those entrusted with church finances are accused of embezzlement. We cry as we learn that someone in the family of God has been sexually or physically harmed. We shake our heads when we hear that the church building down the road has been broken into, damage has been done, and valuables have been taken. We cringe as we listen to the details of a congregation being sued.

Years ago my own family learned of a disturbed church member's plan to abduct our two-year-old son. We recognized that the crime would have been easy to carry out. By God's grace it didn't happen.

As you read this, you may be thinking, *We've never experienced anything like that. Thank God that everything is fine in our congregation.* With that attitude, many congregations continue to be unwise stewards of the buildings, people, and other resources with which they have been entrusted. Though many congregations have become progressive in worship, evangelism, missions, and new building projects, most seem unenlightened in security and safety. Congregations that have been *reactive* rather than *proactive* in dealing with congregational security and safety are learning some difficult lessons.

Instead of sharing the Good News, people embroiled in incidents of poor security and safety are changed in negative ways. Some congregations are split and others close because of lawsuits, accusations, and traumatic events and their aftermath. The once-secure church building has increasingly become a target for thieves. New areas of litigation explored by attorneys often include religious institutions and leaders. No congregation or faith group is immune.

As the Bob Dylan song says, "The times they are a-changin'." The flock is increasingly under attack and forced to defend itself. The monetary and emotional price is rising. And though the frequency and gravity of traumatic incidents are intensifying, we should continue to trust God. We have not been abandoned. God is still in charge. The Lord's care is still promised to us. At the same time, we need to respond faithfully as good stewards of our resources. We may not be able to stop attacks, but there is a good chance that we may be able to reduce their frequency.

As I searched for help for my own congregation, I realized that little comprehensive, user-friendly material was available on the subject of congregational security and safety. As a pastor and a former detective, I believe it is our duty, as undershepherds, to do whatever we can to protect the people and the property God has entrusted to us. As leaders and pastors we are responsible for keeping children and adults safe and secure while they are in our care.

I will acknowledge that security and safety measures, taken to the extreme, could cause us to become something other than the body that Christ meant us to be. I am not suggesting armed guards, metal detectors, or guard towers for a congregation. We should, however, remain a place where people can find trust, love, and acceptance. Our congregations should always strive to provide a place of peace and hope where "the least of these" may find help. Certainly, the balance between maintaining security and nurturing open trust is a delicate one.

This book is designed to help us consider how we might do our best to offer a safe and secure environment for all of God's people. I believe readers will be able to use this book to begin discussing and implementing positive changes in their congregations. Ideally, I hope the congregations whose leaders read this book will adopt comprehensive safety and security policies.

Trust in the Lord, and do good; so you will dwell in the land, and enjoy security (Ps. 37:3, NRSV).

CHAPTER 1

Finances

An inner-city church, a cornerstone of the neighborhood, was left open during the day so that members and friends could come in for quiet and prayer. The custodian, charged with emptying the collection boxes for the poor, noticed that donations were down significantly. Suspecting theft, he installed a camera in the balcony, and a pair of thieves were caught. Both confessed to petty theft.

It is hard to imagine that anyone would want to take the money given for God's work. In the majority of congregations, no one does. But in some—large and small, rural and urban, new and established—theft does take place. Church thefts and burglaries used to be minor, or they went unreported. It's possible that church buildings and religious people, once considered off-limits by most criminals, no longer carry that implied immunity.

Some thefts are carried out by pastors, other employees, or volunteers. These can be petty—small items taken from the church for personal use. Perhaps a custodian takes home toilet paper, light bulbs, and soap. But sophisticated, planned, and ongoing thefts of money are also on the rise in congregations.

The new pastor of one congregation began to sense that something was out of the ordinary about the financial secretary's reporting procedures. When confronted, the secretary became defensive and uncooperative. Later, she stated that a relative had taken the congregation's financial records and destroyed them. Bank authorities and denominational officials were notified. An internal investigation disclosed that the financial secretary was most likely responsible for improper use of the church credit card and unauthorized removal of funds from church accounts, with the total loss estimated at $20,000. No charges were filed.

No confession was offered. No money was recovered. But a new financial secretary was hired.

In cases of internal theft, other issues surface. Those suspected, accused, or caught may be people we have known, trusted, and loved for years. We may have socialized with them, attended a Sunday school class together, or ministered to them. The suspect might be the son of a charter member, or the wife of a board member. He or she may have served the congregation long and faithfully. The accused may even be our pastor. Even to think or whisper of financial indiscretion by the clergy may seem irreverent.

A parish priest was sued by the archdiocese for taking a large amount of money from the congregation he served. The priest's attorney did not deny the charges against his client but sought to have the case settled out of court, with the threat of making embarrassing disclosures about others in the diocese.

Even when the facts are indisputable, we wrestle with whether to fire the culprits, remove them from membership, press criminal charges, force them to pay back the money, or find a way to minister to them. Discussing these issues makes us cringe. We may believe that if we don't talk about such incidents or take action to reduce or eliminate the conditions for theft, it won't happen in our congregation, and we won't have to face the problem. Many others have mistakenly made that assumption. As leaders of congregations, we should take seriously our obligation to protect the people, buildings, and valuables God has entrusted to us. By talking about ways to protect our finances, we can begin putting into place a comprehensive plan covering many areas of safety and security in our congregation.

Chances are that there will never be a theft or embezzlement in your congregation. But the fallout from such an incident is painful, not only affecting the relationships within our church family, but also straining our faith. Many committed religious people have told me that the pain of being a victim was severe and the subsequent recovery slow. The point is this: Taking a few simple steps can prevent such an incident. It still can happen, but preparing for the possibility reduces the risk.

Four key aspects of finances in congregations should be examined:

• Collections, counting, and deposits.
• Check-writing, expenditures, and access to accounts.

• Petty cash.
• Reporting and auditing.

As you scrutinize these areas, remember that each of them applies
in some way to every congregation. The details may differ in your situation, but the suggestions in each section are intended to prompt your
thinking, stimulate discussion, and help you begin looking at your congregation's finances with the shrewdness of a serpent and the innocence
of a dove. Questions at the close of this and subsequent chapters may be
used by congregational leaders to begin the process of making yours a
secure and safe congregation.

Collections, Counting, and Deposits

Armed Robber Makes Off with $6000 Easter Offering.
Man Who Pocketed $240,000 from Church Collections Is Jailed.
Pair Robbed on Way to Deposit Sunday Collection.

How would you like to see one of these headlines in your local paper?
How would you feel if you learned that your congregation's head usher
had been pocketing tens and twenties for years?

How many people in your congregation have access to the offering
from each worship service? Let's walk through a typical worship collection, counting, and deposit process.

At the designated moment, the ushers come forward and begin
working their way up the aisles of the church with the collection plates,
as the organ plays or the choir or congregation sings. Once the collection is finished, the ushers may stand at the back until the Doxology or
some other cue signals them to move to the front of the church. There
the acolytes or the pastor receives the plates and places them on the altar.
The pastor prays over the collection, the ushers return to their places,
and the service continues.

The collection remains up front until the close of the service. As
worshipers stand to leave the church, a designated person—often the
head usher—goes to the front and retrieves the collection plates. The
collection is taken to a designated place (often an office). From there,
the checks and cash may be placed in a bank bag, paper bag, or envelope

and locked in a desk, file, or safe. Or the money may be taken directly
to the bank and placed in the night-deposit box. In some congregations
the offering is counted immediately after worship. Or it may be counted
the following day at the bank, perhaps by the treasurer, finance chair, or
a team of volunteers, and then deposited in the church account.

Let's examine the flaws in such a system. First, after the collection
is taken, the ushers stand at the rear of the nave with the money. For an
outsider who comes to a worship service with the intent to rob, this moment offers a perfect opportunity to grab the money and run. After all,
most eyes are facing the front. The money is amassed in one location,
close to the door.

If the service goes smoothly, the collection is taken to the front of
the sanctuary, where it sits for the remainder of the service. At the close
of worship, people are standing, greeting, and moving about. There's
noise and commotion. The designated person tries to make her way to
the front of the church to retrieve the plates. On the way, people may
wish to greet and speak to her, unwittingly diverting attention from the
plates. Meanwhile, the collection is vulnerable. Others have the opportunity to help themselves to some cash.

Whenever the collection plates are taken to an office to be counted
or locked up, the person who carries the offering is again at risk. First, a
robber now needs to overpower only one person before running out the
door with the cash. Second, any time an individual is alone with the
collection, he is placed in an unwanted position—he may potentially be
accused of theft and have no one to corroborate his story. Although
deeply trusted, he exposes himself to the risk of being suspected falsely.

Congregations use a variety of counting procedures. In some par-
ishes, the collection is counted during or after worship by a team of volunteers—or by the same person each week. The counters most often
work in an office that may or may not be locked. After being counted,
the collection may be locked in a safe or some other secure area and
taken to the bank for deposit the next day. Other congregations choose
to make the deposit immediately. These practices are common in our
congregations. However, in one church, one or another married couple
counted the collection in their home on Sunday afternoon. The designated couple would make the deposit the same day.

Some of the risks are obvious. If counting is done by only one person, or by the same people every week, probably no system is in place to

verify accuracy in counting over a long period. Second, when the same two people usually do the counting and one of them is not available, the task is often done by the other alone.

All counting should take place in a secure area. A high-traffic, highly visible classroom is not secure. A locked office is best. The money should be taken there discreetly, if possible. Once inside, a team—not an individual working alone—should permit no distractions. Team members should work together to verify all entries. They should sign off on the counter's sheet to verify who was present, in case questions arise. Even if the collection is counted at a bank, two unrelated people—not two members of one family—should count it. Teams should be rotated to include a variety of people.

When a deposit is being made, the collection is still at risk. If the counting is done after worship, the process will take some time. By the time the job is completed, most worshipers will have left the building. Probably one or two people will leave the church with a bank bag, envelope, or grocery bag. A thief may watch for this pattern. In one congregation, the same dedicated worker was the last to leave the church building each week. She would cross the town square, bank bag in hand, and place the bag in the bank's night-deposit box—until the unfortunate Sunday when she was hit over the head and the bank bag was taken.

If an especially large collection is expected, it is wise to notify authorities. If great fanfare and publicity have accompanied a fund drive that concludes on a given Sunday, alert criminals might take note as well. Using guards to escort the people with the money to the bank ensures everyone's safety. One congregation that collected more than $2 million in checks and cash on one Sunday had an armored truck and guards waiting just outside the church door.

Whatever the size of the congregation or collection, the objective is to keep the money secure from start to finish, to remove temptation from people whose resistance is low when it comes to easy money, to reduce the opportunity for theft, and to minimize the possibility that anyone might be wrongly accused of theft and unable to muster a defense. Remember, the gifts we collect are a blessing from God, given by the people to be used for God's work. By keeping the gifts secure, we are practicing good stewardship.

Suggestions for Collection, Counting, and Deposits

1. Collected offerings should always be handled by two unrelated people.
2. Those who handle church funds regularly should be bonded.
3. Receipts and disbursements should be handled separately and assigned to different people.
4. Church funds should not be taken to anyone's home.
5. Financial reports should be audited annually, and detailed monthly reports should be kept and reviewed.[1]
6. Follow the entire trail of the collection, observe when it might be at risk and determine what changes might increase security without disrupting the worship service.
7. Immediately after the collection is taken, have at least two alert, able-bodied people take the collection quickly and discreetly to a secure office or safe and lock it up.
8. Rotate the counting teams, and establish a policy that they count the money in a locked area immediately after worship. Document the offering on a standardized form, signed by each counter. Give copies to the financial secretary and others who need them.
9. Direct that two people must always take the collection to be deposited. Have them use different doors to exit the church and alternate routes to the bank each week. Keep the bank bag concealed.
10. Train everyone who handles the collection to follow the procedures outlined in your security and safety plan.
11. Review the plan on a regular basis.

Check-Writing, Expenditures, and Access to Accounts

A financial secretary was occasionally questioned about the incomplete way she reported the congregation's finances. She often became upset and raised her voice to those who asked questions. Few satisfactory answers were forthcoming. Upon investigating, the pastor and lay leaders realized they had a problem. The financial records for the past five years had disappeared; and the audits, scheduled only every other year, had been performed by the financial secretary herself. No one knew how extensive the theft might be. Congregational leaders accepted the financial secretary's resignation and chose not to pursue the matter further.

Embezzlement ranks second only to sexual malfeasance among the most highly visible congregational security and safety issues. Embezzlement can happen in a congregation of any size. Even denominational boards and agencies have lost large sums of money. While some embezzlers take hard cash, adjusting the books is another common way of taking church funds.

Many congregations have re-elected the same financial secretary or treasurer for years. These people have been faithful and trusted volunteers. Never has there been reason to suspect them. Yet we hear of hundreds or thousands of dollars disappearing from churches around the country each year. And these are only the cases that receive headlines. We may suspect that many other cases go undetected or unreported.

Embezzlement takes more planning than stealing cash. Some church officers simply pad various accounts, siphoning off money as bills are paid. For instance, instead of sending $68.00 to pay a bill, the financial secretary may either doctor or destroy the bill, send in more than the amount billed, and receive a refund that never appears on the books. He can then cash the refund check and keep the money.

Other schemes involve a secretary, treasurer, or pastor administering a large discretionary fund. As a pastor, for instance, I have access to a fund to help poor people who come into the church. In our case, I use a form with duplicate copies, giving one copy to the secretary and the original to the recipient. I never deal with cash. But in some congregations people who have access to such funds are required only to make a notation in a journal. Many times the journals are not balanced. Funds are easily diverted for personal use.

Another area of concern is special accounts. Often cash raised at a special event (car wash, dinner, bazaar) is received by the secretary of the sponsoring committee or organization within the congregation. Usually no one has a clue how much was collected. If $275 is deposited in the account instead of the $350 received, no one will know. It is nearly impossible to trace such a transaction. It is more difficult, but not impossible, to embezzle money once it has been deposited in an account.

Some larger cases involve elaborate accounting, bookkeeping, and check-writing schemes. Sometimes dummy accounts or businesses are set up by the offender. Family members may become involved in the scheme, or they may be oblivious to it. Not all cases of embezzlement start out as intended theft. Often we hear of unauthorized borrowing of funds from a congregational account to cover an individual's indebtedness. Fully intending to pay the money back, the borrower never gets around to it or finds that no one notices if the money is not returned. This "borrowing" can begin a long string of cover-ups and lies.

To begin insisting on full and accurate disclosure of accounts is important but may be painful. I spoke to one pastor who admitted that the method of accounting used by his small country congregation was inadequate. But he also recognized that suggested changes would most likely cause the financial secretary to resign and create dissension in the congregation. He was willing to continue the risk rather than upset the members.

In another church, a longtime member with a background in banking oversaw his congregation's special accounts faithfully for years. Included were endowment, memorial, and building funds, and a special-needs fund, of which few church members were aware. When the chair stepped down and retired to Arizona, his successor, a certified public accountant, took over the accounts. Within a short time, the new chair discovered discrepancies in several of the accounts.

Pastors and church members are grateful for the dedicated treasurers and financial secretaries who perform valuable services to congregations. It is important that we give them recognition as often as possible and include them in any discussion about changes in procedure. But we must not be naïve or careless. These are difficult issues in the life of any congregation. When it comes to generating charged emotions, little compares to issues of money. We may want certain people to know or not to know how much we give. Often people donate anonymously or ask that their contribution be made known only to a select person or committee. Disclosure is a touchy matter. But all accounts should be viewed as vulnerable. Extra attention should be paid to special accounts that are used infrequently and seen by few, but that often contain large sums. It is highly recommended that no one person have sole access to an account. Without safeguards, these funds can be misappropriated.

Building in a system of safeguards protects not only the congregation but also those who give of their time to keep the finances in order. The key words are accuracy and accountability. Ongoing, clear, documented accounting is necessary for the church to protect what are sometimes significant amounts of money. Clear written procedures should be adopted and used for all handling of finances.

Suggestions on Check-writing, Expenditures, and Access to Accounts

According to Fred Lawman, former Secret Service agent and professional security consultant, no system is foolproof. In the church, the aim is to reduce the probability of embezzlement. Lawman offers several suggestions in the area of check-writing, expenditures, and access to accounts (the first six items are his):

1. *Dual accounting.* At a minimum, income is recorded by one person and banking done by another. Books should be reviewed, if possible, by a third party.
2. *Regular audits.* Periodic and unannounced audits should be performed by people not directly associated with any of the funds.
3. *Dual checking and savings.* Consider requiring two signatures on all checks and withdrawals.
4. *Background checks.* Though distasteful to many, routine background checks should be considered for anyone who will be handling money or accounts. Procedures differ from state to state. Some churches conduct both criminal and financial checks. Releases from those to be checked out are required.
5. *Computer financial programs.* Financial software programs such as Quicken, Quickbooks, and Money (and there are others) permit easy review of the books. Irregularities are more easily spotted than with the use of traditional ledger systems. This software is available at most computer software stores.
6. *Personal counseling and training.* Church members should be afforded professional counseling and training about financial problems and solutions. (Many embezzlers are people with personal money problems.)[2]
7. *Back-up finance people.* Ensure that more than one person is familiar with the record-keeping system. This practice is important for at least two reasons, the first being the issue of accountability. Second, if something suddenly happens to the treasurer, someone can step in with the knowledge needed to maintain continuity.
8. *Use of guidelines.* Written guidelines should be familiar to everyone who handles any account.
9. *Term limits.* Consider rotating financial people. Setting terms for those who handle the finances not only prevents burnout but also lets

everyone know that leaders are working to ensure that the congregation's finances are cared for.

10. *Pastors and money.* Don't let the pastor handle the books. This is a sensitive issue in many congregations, but pastors who handle cash, checkbooks, and accounts are setting themselves up for trouble. The need for accountability and avoiding even the appearance of misconduct should be enough to deter pastors from assuming such a role.

11. *Central location.* Consider a central treasury for the congregation, so that all financial transactions are handled from one location. The more individual accounts, the greater the chance of misconduct. Besides, it is good stewardship not to pay service charges for maintaining multiple accounts.

12. *Policies for reporting.* Use a full-disclosure method of reporting. Require the financial secretary and treasurer to keep the congregation informed of exactly where the church stands. Allow no secrets about anything other than individual members' giving and employees' salaries. The trust level of the members increases when everything is disclosed.

Petty Cash

"I need to run down to the office supply store and pick up a few things for the office," the pastor says to the secretary. "Can I have some petty cash to cover it?" With that, the pastor opens the petty cash box, helps herself to a $20 bill, and heads off to the store. By the time she returns, the secretary has gone for the day. The pastor deposits the change and the receipt in the petty cash box.

Has the pastor done anything wrong? Not necessarily. She took money out and returned the change with a receipt. All should be in order. But is it?

The first issue that arises in relation to petty cash is location. Is the money kept in the secretary's desk? In the file cabinet? In a cigar box? In a locked box? Is the cash always secure when the secretary must leave the office?

Next, who has access to petty cash? Is someone in charge of the box? Should anyone other than the pastoral staff and a secretary have access? Most petty cash boxes contain coins, bills, and a large pile of receipts. Normally, losses from petty cash are never missed. But consider what happens if a person takes just $5 a week. Over five years, $1,200 would have been stolen. Wise stewards can't allow such a risk. If the pastor takes a $20 bill to buy office supplies, who would know, other than the pastor, that the change was ever returned? She needs to protect herself from false allegations or suspicions.

We need also to ask about the system for balancing the petty cash. Is it a weekly routine? Monthly? Is a receipt required when cash is removed? Is any notation required regarding cash taken?

Finally, consider the amount kept in petty cash. Many churches try to maintain a predetermined amount in the box. When the cash dips below a certain level, the person in charge requests money or writes a check to bring it up to the original amount. Should there be $50? $100? More? Large amounts of available cash mean that a loss can be more than petty. Robbers who enter your church building during office hours will most often be looking for cash. It's best to have only a minimal amount available. Instruct office workers confronted by a robber to give up the cash. It is never worth risking the life of a staff person for the sake of money.

Chances are that a congregation will never have to declare bankruptcy because of the mishandling or theft of petty cash. But with a sloppy system in place, we may place temptation before people or open the possibility of a false accusation that cannot be refuted. With a secure system in operation, the chances of loss are minimized.

Suggestions for a Petty Cash System

1. Consider keeping petty cash somewhere other than the secretary's desk. That's the first place a thief who breaks in or a robber who uses force will look. In any case, the box should always be locked, and it should be kept in a locked drawer or cabinet.
2. Ideally, one person should have the duty of dispensing the money and keeping accurate records. Every transaction should be recorded in a ledger so that money taken out and change returned are documented. Transactions should be backed up with a receipt.
3. Balance the petty-cash box at regular intervals. On the first workday

of the month, for instance, the person in charge should remove or add to the total cash on hand, take out the receipts, and begin with the specific amount needed for the month. Ideally, this routine takes place in the presence of a witness. Question discrepancies if the receipts and cash don't add up. Put the receipts in a safe place, at least until audits are conducted on the petty-cash account.

4. Establish procedures for the permissible uses of petty cash and the maximum amount that may be removed at one time. Larger purchases should be handled with a voucher system, not petty cash.

5. Minimize the number of people, including members, who see the person in charge go into the petty cash box. No one needs to know where the box is kept, especially the stranger who comes in off the street asking for assistance. Smart criminals make notes for the future. It is better to ask those who come in for assistance to wait somewhere away from the office while you conduct the necessary business.

6. Consider asking staff and volunteers to pay for minor purchases and bring in the receipt for reimbursement. Then the receipt can be put into the box and a notation made in the ledger.

7. Clarify and discuss the guidelines for handling petty cash with those who deal with it.

Reporting and Auditing

A neglected and less obvious area of congregational financial management is reporting and auditing. I have found that most members of a congregation don't read the monthly financial reports. Most couldn't say with assurance whether an audit is done. Therefore, it falls to a few people to ensure that reports and audits are done responsibly.

Numerous reporting and auditing methods have been explained to me in the course of my research. Some were good. Others were terrible. One church, to save money, decided that the financial report should be given only to five key people in the congregation. No one else knew the status of the church's finances, except for what could be gleaned from an occasional verbal report at a board meeting.

Other congregations conduct an internal audit, either as a requirement of their denomination or because they believe it is the right thing to do. But even these audits span the spectrum from professional and thorough to more-or-less cursory.

The purpose of reporting is disclosure. Keeping members informed of the congregation's financial condition, whether they are interested or not, says to them, "We have nothing to hide." Let's face it: Some people do not have a high trust level in regard to the church's handling of their finances. Disclosure allows everyone to see what's going on. Monthly statements should have a clear opening and closing balance, a running tally of the money received and spent to date, and a statement indicating where the congregation stands on the annual budget. At a minimum, a summary of the various areas of the budget should be made available.

The objective of auditing is protection. Audits help us fulfill our responsibility to protect both the finances and the people who handle them. The cursory audit most often is conducted by a person or group of people (sometimes the finance committee) charged with reviewing all church accounts on a regular (most often annual) basis. Sometimes the review consists of running a tape of the account to see if it balances.

More complete audits are preferred. The auditor may be a certified public accountant (CPA) or a financially trained person within the congregation. Such audits should not be done by the financial secretary or treasurer. Objectivity is necessary. An even more thorough audit may be performed by an outside agency. Larger congregations with bigger budgets should seriously consider scheduling an outside audit annually. Smaller churches may wish to have an internal audit done annually and a more complete outside audit every few years.

Another increasingly popular way to keep the books in order is to move from written ledgers to a computerized system. The systems now available to churches can do everything from monitoring and reporting offerings to writing checks. Using such a method centralizes congregational finances and reduces the opportunity to change the books manually. Such a system reduces the chances of embezzlement.

The line between financial mismanagement and embezzlement is not always clear. What looks like sloppy reporting and management may be just that—or it may be a scheme to siphon money. In either case, it is important to remind ourselves of our responsibility as faithful stewards to protect the people and the assets of our congregation. This duty means ensuring that our system does not make it easy for people to be tempted or to be successful in obtaining funds for their own use.

Suggestions for Reporting and Auditing

1. Consider rotating treasurers. This practice may be difficult for a small church that has few qualified people available to keep the books. Even asking two people to rotate occasionally would help.
2. When auditing, be sure you see the original checkbook, checks, and records.
3. Run a total for an account at random. At various times audit a single line item, checking the payments, receipts, check stubs, and signatures.
4. Store canceled checks and books at the church.
5. Always appoint two unrelated persons to count offerings, serve as treasurer and financial secretary, and handle money.[3]
6. Conduct a complete audit on a regular basis. Use financially astute members or outside agencies. A thorough audit offers peace of mind for all involved.
7. Make a monthly financial report available in some form to the congregation. What may be hidden from a few may be obvious to many. An attitude that there is nothing to hide fosters congregational trust.
8. Use a computer system for all financial dealings.
9. Require a voucher system for purchases, and save receipts.
10. Seek to foster a sense of cooperation in regard to congregational finances.

A System of Accountability

In many ways, the members of our congregations are a reflection of society. The very nature of God's church should cause us to invite the broken and imperfect into our midst. Many times we are able to work with them toward healing and wholeness. But sometimes we place those in the process of restoration and healing in areas of service that put them and us at risk. The symptoms of their problems often manifest themselves in some area of congregational life. For a person who has a gambling problem, some areas of service would be appropriate, but working with finances would not. It is good to involve troubled people in ministries, but we must be cautious in designating the areas where we ask them to serve.

Though we sometimes expose ourselves to these symptoms and

risks, we can also take steps to reduce the chances for loss. Like it or not, money is often society's measure of success. Those who don't have money look for ways to get it. Those who do have it sometimes want more. As a congregation, we should do everything in our power to safeguard the gifts of money that come to us from members and visitors, as well as to protect the people who handle our finances.

The vast majority of people who deal with congregational finances are trustworthy and dedicated. I thank God for them. Let's keep them safe by creating a system of accountability that will glorify God and lower our anxiety level about church finances.

Questions for Self-Evaluation

1. Do we have a clear, written procedure for collections?
2. Have our ushers been trained to carry out those procedures?
3. Are our collections safe from robbers? Are the people who handle the offering protected from the appearance of possible misconduct?
4. Do at least two unrelated people handle the collection as a team from the time it is received until it is deposited?
5. Do we rotate the collection counters?
6. Do we have in place an adequate collection reporting procedure? Is it followed?
7. Do we use safe procedures for taking money to the bank?
8. Is our petty cash kept in a discreet and secure location? Is a balance system used?
9. Do we use a receipt, voucher, or some other type of secure system to make purchases?
10. Are our books kept at the church, filled out in ink, and made available to those who have a legitimate need to see them?
11. Do we require two people to sign checks, or is the person in charge of check-writing rotated periodically?
12. Have we computerized our finances?
13. Do we schedule regular, complete audits on our general account?
14. Do we conduct background checks and bond those who handle our finances?
15. Are audits conducted and reports filed on special accounts, investments, and stocks?
16. Could our church offer financial training and counseling?

17. When should we begin discussions with everyone involved in con-
    gregational finances that will move us toward a comprehensive
    safety and security policy?
18. Have we prayed about this issue?

CHAPTER 2

Building Security

Arriving at the church one morning, the pastor found the main door un-locked. Intruders had broken into the offices. The sanctuary had also been ransacked. Missing were new computers, most of the sound system, televisions, VCRs, and petty cash. There were no signs of forced entry. Asked who had access to the church building, the pastor admitted, "Just about everyone." The crime was never solved.

We will examine five areas of concern for church building security. The first is illustrated above—access. Churches need to protect their buildings from the negligence or misconduct of current or former members, and ensure that people can't use the building without church leaders' knowledge.

Many churches simply don't know who has access to their buildings. In one church I served, a mysterious copy-machine bandit made hundreds of copies after hours. The thief was never caught. We responded by changing the locks on the office door. Many church secretaries and pastors say they have no accurate process for getting borrowed or assigned keys back. One pastor told me, "I suspect half the people in our community have access to our church."

The next threat concerns outside groups that use our church. Most congregations believe that their facilities should be accessible to individuals and groups in the community. It is not uncommon for one or more groups to be renting their space or using it without charge. Access of such groups introduces a potential breakdown in security. We should ask how well we know those who have access to our church buildings. Imagine a pastor's surprise when she arrived at church to find a group she did not recognize using the building. Scanning the church calendar, she saw no group listed for that time slot. Checking further, she learned that a trustee had, on his own authority, given his key to an acquaintance who asked to use the church. Security had been compromised. Even if authorization is given, there should be a clear, understood, secure process for opening and closing the building.

Another area of security risk involves thieves. Burglars looking to make a fast buck may find churches an easy mark. A congregation in the Southeast found itself a victim of burglary not once but twice in two weeks. Burglars pried open the church doors, entered the building, and stole money from the poor boxes. Despite the installation of an extra lock, the thieves broke in again through the same door and again took money from the poor boxes. Only after the second break-in did congregational officials consider installing steel doors and windows and a security system.

Sometimes the loss is much higher than money taken from a collection box for the poor. Bibles, choir robes, and hymnals aren't big-ticket items on the black market, but complete sound and computer systems, televisions, VCRs, and musical equipment are. With increasing regularity, burglars and robbers are recognizing that congregations are not, for the most part, doing a good job of securing their buildings and locking up valuables. The first steps are to keep intruders out of the building and to secure our belongings inside.

Church buildings can also be used as a place of rest for homeless people. Those who have nowhere else to stay may look to the church to provide a safe, dry, warm place of refuge. They may come and ask for permission to sleep in the building. But they may also look for an open door or an unlocked window after hours. Once inside, they may just sleep. But they may also look for clothing, food, and valuables easily turned into cash.

Another category of intruders consists of people who come not to steal but to desecrate. A growing number of individuals and groups apparently want to bring down faith communities. They desire to dishonor our God. Though not nearly so prevalent as vagrancy, theft, and unsecured buildings, vandals and satanic groups that violate houses of worship are on the rise. Some congregations take steps to upgrade security by changing security procedures. Others address the issue with security alarm systems. And yet others do not want to discuss the issue. They take a naïve, out-of-sight, out-of-mind view and assume, "If we don't talk about it, it won't happen to us."

A number of approaches can be taken to make our buildings more secure. Five areas form the core of congregational response to the building-security issue.

Member Access

The choir rehearses every Wednesday evening from 7:30 to 8:30. Usually the music director unlocks the building as she arrives and locks up when she leaves. On one particular Wednesday the church is unlocked as usual at 7:15. The choir arrives at 7:30, along with the youth board, which has scheduled a meeting that night. At 8:30 the choir finishes practicing, and as the director leaves at 8:45, she notices that the youth board is still in session. Therefore, she does not lock the door. At 9:15 the youth board members finish their meeting and leave. Since they did not unlock the building, they feel no responsibility for locking up. The church is left unlocked. At 2:30 A.M. the pastor receives a call to come to the church to secure the door—from the police, who in some communities routinely check for unlocked doors.

What can a congregation do to secure its building and still make the space available to members? Planning for building security is easy, but putting a plan into operation and maintaining it takes work. The place to start is access. To provide easy access to various groups and people from our congregation, we usually hand out keys. Considering the number of leaders who rotate through our committees each year, we can estimate that within a few years, hundreds of keys are "out there." Without a system in place to collect and monitor keys no longer needed, the church building is extremely vulnerable. Still, many church people dislike asking outgoing leaders to return their keys. Like asking an about-to-be-fired corporate manager for the keys to the executive rest room, retrieving keys from a person who is no longer an appointed or elected leader of the congregation can be awkward. Negative responses are not uncommon. One woman, who no longer held a position in the congregation, read in the church newsletter that we were collecting keys from former leaders. She came in and threw her key down on the secretary's desk and walked out in a huff. But the expectation of angry responses should not deter us from implementing a policy for church access.

Along with providing, collecting, and monitoring keys, we should also address the attitudes that impinge on building security. Some congregational leaders tell me that they keep the church open all day, whether or not anyone is on the premises. They want to provide easy access for members. Too often, "It's too much of a hassle" describes the prevailing attitude. When people need access to the church, the operative word is "convenience." If they are out and around and need to check on something or pick up an item at the church, they want to do it on their time and schedule. Instead of planning to come when the church is open, they would prefer to have a key. Convenience often wins out over security.

Even when we have policies stating who is responsible for unlocking and locking the doors and have an adequate key policy, we need to decide who should have access to specific areas of the building. Do we want all members to have access to the church office? The pastor's office? The financial records? I can't imagine that we do. Different keys should provide access to the specific areas that people with specific responsibilities need to enter. The only people with keys should be those who absolutely need access. For instance, I do not believe that all cleaning and paper supplies, tools, and custodial products should be easily accessible to the general congregation. Adequate supplies, equipment, and tools should be made available to everyone, but objects that tend to be taken should be secured.

Granting access to the church office or pastor's office may mean that we are also providing access to church equipment and confidential records in files or on the computer. When I did not have a filing cabinet that locked, I felt that my records were fairly secure, as my office door always remained locked—that is, until I began finding notes and small gifts on my desk. I realized I needed to take steps to secure my office. I had the lock changed and acquired a locking file cabinet. Keeping donation records, petty cash, and personnel and counseling files secure is essential.

It is important that members know that we want them to have the access they need to the church building. It is equally important that we educate them on the necessity of securing the church and being good stewards of God's building and its contents.

Suggestions for Member Access

1. Issue a set number of church keys, each stamped with a number and the words "Do Not Duplicate." Maintain a list of who has each numbered key. Keep all extra keys secure.
2. Have a clearly understood process for distributing keys and collecting them from those who no longer need them. Make it someone's responsibility.
3. Change the locks every three to four years. Advertise the change to the congregation well in advance.
4. Let the staff, congregational leaders, and members know who is responsible for unlocking and locking the building.
5. Keep the congregation informed and educated. If there are problems or changes in building-security procedures, let members know so that they can respond.
6. Use codes to access computers and copy machines.
7. Make sure members know to notify the police if there will be late-night or overnight activities at the church. (Imagine the surprise of our youth group members when they were startled by two police officers who entered the building with flashlights and guns drawn after finding the church unlocked.)

Outside Groups

The local Red Cross had for several years used your church building for its classes in cardiopulmonary resuscitation (CPR). A key was given to the group, and group leaders took care of opening and closing the building. Then the group decided to move to another building across town. Several months after the Red Cross ceased using your building, someone asked, "Did we ever get our key back?"

A local political group needs a place to meet. Some members of the congregation are also members of the group and ask if the meetings may be held at your church. Permission is granted, and you give a key to one of your members and tell him that he is responsible for opening the building and locking up afterward.

A young couple wants to get married in your church because the church they regularly attend is too small for a large wedding. They fill out the standard church-usage form. After your pastor speaks to theirs, the wedding is scheduled. Your custodian opens up the building several hours before the wedding. He returns as the wedding guests are leaving, cleans up, and locks the doors. The next day, several microphones are missing. Where do you turn?

Each of these stories points to problems involved in allowing outside individuals and groups to use the church building. Most congregations like to offer the use of their space, either without charge or for a fee, to outside groups in the community. Reaching out connects us with others beyond our walls. But without proper safeguards, we leave our congregation at risk. We must count the cost.

As with our own members, it is critical to have a system in place for disbursing and collecting keys. We need to know which person from each group has a key. A group that used our building rotated leadership each quarter. After finding doors left unlocked several times, I tried to call the person who made the original contact with us and to whom we had given a key. I found that she was no longer associated with the group. It took me several weeks to get in touch with the current president. This incident did not show good management on our part.

Political groups present other concerns. How do we know the issues in which they are involved? Do their concerns coincide with what the church stands for? Could the IRS view us as having a connection with them? If so, our nonprofit status could be put in jeopardy. Some churches allow any group to use their facilities for free. Others charge a rental fee. For a variety of reasons, it may be wise to rent, even for a minimal charge. Free usage can imply that the group has a connection to your church—if not in the eyes of the government, at least in the eyes of the community. You may also want to consider whether the group using your church is a "for profit" entity (for example, a day-care provider or other business). That fact could affect your nonprofit status as well.

If outside groups are using your church, what recourse do you have when something is broken or missing? Very little, unless a clear set of guidelines is in place to ensure accountability. If the day after an event you find something not as it should be, you may ask the police to investigate. Or you may call the renting parties to see if they have an explanation. But you may have to chalk it up to the cost of being in ministry to the community. A person or group can easily deny involvement. People may accurately contend that they are not in charge of the security of the entire building while they are using a portion of it.

For this reason, it is vital to have written procedures and a completed usage form indicating who will open and close the building, what activities will take place, how many people are expected to attend, what areas of the church will be used, who is the responsible party, and whether a security deposit has been charged. It is then up to the congregation to follow through. If the custodian is responsible for opening and closing the building, perhaps the group should be required to pay for his presence during the activity. If the custodian inspects the premises before the group leaves, this procedure also ensures the group that it will not be charged for damage caused by someone else. If the outside group is required to close up the building and it is found open or objects are missing or broken, little can be done.

In addition, those from outside the church are probably more likely than a member to bring a lawsuit against the congregation should they be injured in your church. Courts in many states agree that congregations must meet a higher standard of care for those whom we invite to use our church than for our own members. Standard care should be provided for all, but extra care is needed for nonmembers and invited guests to reduce risk.

There is a delicate balance to be preserved between ensuring security and providing access to people and groups that want to use the church building. I hope that we don't reach the point of denying access to anyone not associated with the congregation. By educating ourselves and implementing a plan, we may be able to have the best of both worlds.

Suggestions on Church Access for Outside Groups

1. Design usage forms to be completed by every group using the church building. Ask for the name of the group, contact person, purpose of meeting, space and equipment needs, and hours of use. Ask whether the group has its own insurance. Include guidelines that the group representative must read and sign.
2. Make sure that keys are returned after use.
3. If outside groups carry no insurance of their own, ask your insurer whether your policy covers accidents or loss that results from the group's usage.
4. Have a written policy specifying what types of groups may use your church building and for what purposes.

5. Consider protecting your building and valuables by asking groups to pay a fee for a custodian or caretaker who remains in the building during their activity.

Thieves and Vagrants

Some years ago, before my arrival as pastor, many houses of worship in our community were broken into over an extended period of time. Ours was among them. The favored items of the thieves were sound systems. They recklessly tore equipment from the walls and out of cabinets. Items taken included speakers, amplifiers, microphones, and sound mixer boards. It is not unusual for a string of similar break-ins to occur in one area.

The most sought-after items on the black market are sound equipment, computer equipment, precious art and sculpture, and any easily sold valuables. We should not leave these things in a visible or marked location.

Cash is also highly desired. The church office is usually where thieves look for it. Experienced break-in artists realize that many faith communities do little to protect their valuables and to secure their buildings.

Crimes against congregations are also becoming more bold. In one synagogue on a Saturday night, while a wedding was taking place, thieves jimmied a lock, broke into the office, and hauled out a safe weighing between 800 and 1,000 pounds. It contained just $25 in cash.

In another congregation, thieves entered undetected during office hours, found a hiding place, waited until the secretary left the office, went in and stole her unsecured purse containing a large amount of money, and fled. She estimated that she was out of the office for less than five minutes.

We must realize that robbers may get in regardless of the measures we take. But why make it easy? We need to do what we can to slow the robber down and aid in apprehension, should a break-in occur. By securing valuables in unmarked, locked locations and indelibly marking the equipment, we can achieve this aim.

While researching this guide, I came across several stories that started out badly and ended well. In one case police received a tip about a suspect in a recent series of Christmastime church burglaries. They found their suspect, who first denied the charges. Police then showed him a security videotape from one of the churches, on which he appeared. He not only confessed to the police but asked to confess to the priest of the parish as well.

Another group of people with whom congregations deal are local homeless people, or vagrants. As I was locking up after a meeting, I was startled to find a man inside the church. He told me he was looking for a rest room to use as he made his way across the country. I allowed him to use the rest room, and offered to pay for a room at a nearby hotel. He refused the offer. I locked the building, saw him on his way, and went home. I still don't know what his intentions were.

My heart goes out to those who have no home. We should always work together with other churches and community groups to help them with their shelter needs. But in so doing, we don't need to place ourselves obviously in harm's way or expose our buildings and valuables to theft, if faithful and economically sound precautions can prevent misfortune.

Suggestions Regarding Thieves and Vagrants

1. Inspect and secure or replace unsecured windows and doors.
2. Keep entrances and areas around windows and doors free from bushes that will conceal a thief. Use adequate outside lighting.
3. Lock up all electronic equipment in unmarked closets.
4. Record the model and serial numbers, value, and purchase dates of all equipment, and keep this information in a file. Consider inscribing the equipment and making a videotaped inventory.
5. Lock up expensive china, silver, and communion sets in unmarked drawers or cabinets. Don't advertise the location of valuables.
6. Train sound technicians, audiovisual people, and band members to secure their equipment.
7. Once an inventory is taken, check with your insurance company to make sure you have adequate coverage. See if equipment kept in the building but owned by members is covered as well.
8. Ask police to make frequent patrols of the building and property.
9. Use a security sticker provided by your alarm company. If you don't

have a security system, consider placing something that looks like an alarm sticker on your window. Most thieves won't get close enough to read it.

Hate and Anti-Religious Groups

Arriving one Saturday to clean the church, the custodian found a note taped to the door. The crudely written message said that the next day a satanic group planned to visit the church to observe the Sunday worship service. The note stated that the group meant no harm and simply wanted to observe. Once notified, the pastor called a member of the congregation who was a local police officer. Although few people were made aware of the message left by the group, that Sunday armed plainclothes police were present in worship for the first time in anyone's memory. Their presence gave those who knew an uneasy feeling. The expected satanic visitors did not show up.

While many people break into church buildings mainly to steal money and equipment, others enter for the primary purpose of desecrating a house of worship, sometimes with a secondary purpose of theft. Sometimes the primary motive is difficult to determine.

Five rural churches in one county were burglarized in the same month. Though the items taken included VCRs, televisions, sound systems and cash, one church experienced an additional shock. The pastor found a note left in her office—a threat against her life containing satanic language. The five churches jointly offered a $1,000 reward. Two nights later, the television and VCR were returned with a note of apology. Soon afterward, a young man was arrested for theft and vandalism.

Let's face it: there are groups that hate religious people. They teach and promote hate and violence against communities of faith simply for the fact that we call ourselves faithful. Other thugs burn churches simply because of the skin color of the people who worship there.

Other groups attack our people and buildings for a social stance taken by our denomination or the local congregation. Preaching against a local video store that rents pornographic movies, accepting or excluding homosexuals, taking a stance either against or for abortion—these are just a few of the issues that can push the buttons of individuals and loose-knit hate groups. Seldom do well-organized and publicized groups take such measures as vandalizing, desecrating, or burning houses of worship or sending hate mail. I do not suggest that we should back away from controversial issues. But I do advocate considering the possible ramifications of involvement before taking such stances.

One of the better security programs I have found is the Church-Watch Program developed in Pulaski, Tennessee. It involves the police and congregations in identifying steps to be taken to prevent church arson and other hate crimes against religious institutions. Where we fall on the social or religious spectrum is not the point. We need to be aware that our stances may bring us threats and harm. Identifying the risks and taking measures to discourage people from acting on threats and misguided thinking is something we can all do. There is a delicate balance between speaking out in faith against those practices that we believe go against God's will and placing our church and congregation at risk.

Suggestions for Dealing with Hate or Anti-religious Groups

1. No threat should be taken lightly. If a phone call or letter threatens the well-being of an individual or the church building itself, notify authorities. Let them assess the risk. Other congregations may have received similar threats.
2. If a threat or unusual note arrives, discuss it with a few key leaders in the congregation. It may not be in the church's best interest to let every member know immediately. If there is a specific threat, it is important to weigh the cost of canceling worship services or a meeting to protect the lives of members. Solicit wise counsel from police, key leaders, and pastoral staff.
3. If a threat comes by phone, either record the conversation (if possible) or write down as much of it as you can. Ask for clarity, and listen for common phrases, unusual words, accents, and background noises. When the caller hangs up, call the police immediately, especially when harm to property or an individual is threatened.
4. If a threat seems immediate—such as, "I am on the way to your church to kill everyone!"—get everyone out of the building. The key is to respond quickly and calmly.
5. If no threat is aimed directly at your congregation or a member but you become aware of increased threats, burglaries, vandalism, or

arson in your area, you may want to organize a "church-watch" program. This plan involves members intentionally driving past the church whenever they are out and about. Ask them to circle the church a few times and to look for unlocked doors or broken windows. If something seems wrong, they should not enter the church but rather inform police or a church official of their findings.

Security Alarm Systems

Finally, churches may consider a building security system. As I spoke to pastors and church administrators, I found that most smaller and older congregations were unwilling to buy into the concept or to allocate the money for a security system. It is understandable that many smaller churches pride themselves on being open, intimate, trusting fellowships. But larger and newer congregations seem to accept security systems as a way of life. I will continue to stress the need for unobtrusive, easy-to-access security measures for congregations. A 24-hour armed guard with a metal detector and an attack dog at every door would be a deterrent to crime. But who wants to see that level of security at the entrance of a church building? Security systems may provide the best unobtrusive method available. They range from elaborate and expensive to adequate and affordable. You can get a system wired to every door and window, or one that includes motion detectors. You can even get the sound of a dog barking in reaction to glass breaking or a loud noise.

Many systems sold by security companies are wired in such a way that a central office is alerted to an alarm and within moments can assess the authenticity of the alarm and notify police, fire, or emergency personnel. Most systems no longer notify local authorities directly. There is a monthly fee for the company's service. In addition, some municipalities charge businesses, homeowners, and congregations for more than a set number of alarms in a given time frame.

Security systems might also include a coded entry system or two-way voice communication whereby those entering the building would enter a code to release the door latch or speak into an intercom to have it manually released. However, I admit that problems arise in the life of the church when people are asked to change their current habits, undergo training, and follow new procedures. Many desire access, and few like the hassle of remembering a code. These are some of the trade-offs a congregation must consider.

Some congregations have also installed security cameras. They may be used only during the day or around the clock. The monitors are most often located in the church office. Some systems can be installed by mechanically inclined church members. The cost is reasonable. A monitor system also has the capacity to record, a helpful feature after hours or for monitoring nursery or children's areas.

Security alarm systems can also include fire-, smoke- and flood-detection equipment. Some church buildings have smoke alarms, but if no one is inside the church to hear them after hours, how much damage could happen before someone becomes aware of the smoke or fire? Finally, a "panic button," to be used by an individual being robbed or suffering a medical emergency, is an available option.

For an adequate assessment of needs, it is advisable to contact a reputable security alarm company or security consultant. Check competency by asking leaders of congregations that are customers. Ask the company about its longevity in the business, and ask if its monitoring company is UL (Underwriters Laboratory) listed (a standard in the business). Reputable consultants know the right questions to ask and can help with an overall plan. I also encourage using your insurance carrier as a resource. The company should have loss-prevention information and personnel to assist you. It is in the insurer's best interest to help your congregation to prevent a loss.

Suggestions for Security Alarm Systems

1. Invite police, fire, insurance, and security professionals into your building to offer advice.
2. Consider a security alarm system with programmable entry codes. Train those who need to have access to the church. Change codes as needed when too many people have access.
3. Select a reputable, researched alarm company. Don't hesitate to ask another congregation about its system and monitoring company.
4. Consider installing security cameras in strategic locations throughout your church.
5. Since this change will affect the entire congregation, discuss the

issue of a security system with as many people as possible. Become
educated and plan together.

Securing God's House

Some congregations will choose to do little or nothing to upgrade building security and safety, hoping to remain in an earlier era perceived as
safer. By avoiding the issues and remaining oblivious to the rising risk
congregations face, they may feel secure. But as I speak to congregational leaders and members who have suffered a break-in, robbery, theft,
desecration, or other criminal incident, each one voices regrets at not
having done more. They recognized that their approach was incomplete
and that they were left vulnerable.

Other congregations have recognized the need to secure their buildings and to adopt a comprehensive plan. They have begun educating
themselves through the few organizations that deal with church security
and safety issues, or with information from their insurance company or
denomination. These congregations acknowledge that securing their
building, valuables, and people costs money, but they see that the price
of a loss is potentially much higher. They also recognize that a safe and
secure building is an effective method of attracting and retaining families looking for a congregational home.

Maybe your congregation stands somewhere in between. You recognize the need to become more security-conscious. You have concluded
that the security of the church building is as important as the security
you desire in your home. You know that this is God's house, and you
have a desire to treat it as such. Still, you aren't sure how to begin, what
to do, and where to turn.

By securing the building and protecting your assets, your congregation will take a large step forward in the area of church security and
safety. A safe and secure, unobtrusive congregational security environment is possible to achieve. And yet, people should still be able to see
their church as an inviting place. The key is open, honest dialogue with
everyone involved. Hear the concerns and formulate a policy that is best
for the congregation, recognizing that no decision will please everyone.

If you establish a policy based on informed, practical principles
rather than personalities, administration of the policy can be carried out
in a more acceptable and uniform way over the long haul.

Questions for Self-Evaluation

1. Do we have a disbursement and collection policy for keys? Is the congregation aware of it? Where do we keep the list of key-holders and the extra keys?
2. Do we know who has access to the offices and equipment in our church?
3. What group within our congregation sets policy and makes changes on issues of security and access? How well is this group doing its job?
4. Do we plan ahead when a congregational or outside group needs access to the church? Who is responsible for opening the building and locking up?
5. Do we require a usage form to be completed by groups within the congregation? Do we know what areas they will be using and what activities they will be engaged in? Do we know who is the responsible party?
6. Have we inspected windows, doors, offices, and storage areas inside the building? Are they secure? Have we had any problems? Is our equipment too vulnerable and accessible? Could we begin by securing these areas?
7. Might we form a security-minded team, trained in awareness of potential problems, that will inspect and look for problems the rest of the congregation might not see?
8. Have we given permission to church neighbors to report suspicious activities?
9. Is a church-watch program possible in our congregation?
10. Do we have a complete inventory of equipment that includes model and serial numbers and purchase dates? Is our equipment indelibly marked with an identification number? Could someone make a videotaped inventory?
11. Is a security alarm system possible now or in the future? How might we fund it?
12. Could we purchase and install cameras?
13. Do we use security codes for computers and other equipment?
14. Are we certain that our insurance carrier will cover all losses? When items are donated or purchased, do we check our policy to make sure the newly acquired items are covered?

15. Could we invite professionals (police, fire, insurance, and security specialists) to give us direction?

CHAPTER 3

Building Safety

It was a beautiful spring day for the women's group's annual spring luncheon. Most of the women had been coming to the luncheon faithfully for decades. This year the award to the oldest attending member would be presented to Mrs. Sonoff. Now 91 years old, she had attended her first spring luncheon 63 years ago.

As Mrs. Sonoff entered the building, she reached for the handrail to steady herself as she walked down to the lower level. She was fine for two steps. But as she leaned her weight on the handrail, it suddenly pulled away from the wall. Mrs. Sonoff fell down the small flight of stairs, and the handrail struck her head as she landed. Though others were close by, no one was able to prevent the accident.

An ambulance was called, and Mrs. Sonoff went to the hospital with bruises, cuts, and a broken leg. The spring luncheon was a flop. Questions were raised as to who was responsible. Church officials determined, after questioning numerous people and reviewing the minutes of the trustees' meeting, that the need for repair of the handrail had first been raised three months ago. In subsequent months the handrail had been discussed further, but no one "got around" to repairing it.

The physical conditions of our church buildings can cause us concern. If needed repairs are deferred, members and visitors can be exposed to potential harm and the congregation to significant liability. In many states the care of invitees carries a much higher level of liability than the care of regular attendees. The outsiders are in unfamiliar surroundings and less aware of hazards in the church building.

In any case, hazards often arise without warning, caused by inclement weather, equipment malfunctions, spills, inadequate workmanship, or an aging building. Putting in place systems to deal with hazards quickly and effectively can significantly reduce injury and liability. At the very least, a hazard should be marked in an obvious way to warn people of the danger.

In far too many congregations, hazardous conditions and needed repairs are not addressed quickly. This delay isn't always due to neglect. Many faith communities rely on volunteer or part-time help. Not all congregations have a caretaker on the premises around the clock. But when an unstable condition is noted, congregations that do not respond immediately have opened the door to a variety of problems.

The annual community Christmas performance of Handel's *Messiah* was held at First Church on an especially nasty December day. Snow had fallen, then melted, and slush was tracked through the church. Not surprisingly, no one tried to mop up the melted snow. The crowd was large, and extra chairs were needed. One visitor, acting on her own, went to the basement to get a chair, slipped on the stairway, and injured her back. She requested that the congregation pay her extensive medical bills. The church refused, citing obvious hazardous conditions and the fact that the woman had entered an area not open to those attending the concert. The woman sued, but before the case could go to trial, the insurance company settled with her.

In dealing with building safety, we must consider members, volunteers, visitors, policies, and coverage. Most church buildings in this country are much older than 25 years, and with age come hazards. Considering the human factor and the age of the buildings, we can see that if we are not actively looking into potential safety issues, we are negligent. Should an incident cause injury, chances are that liability will fall on our congregation, its leaders and officers, the pastors, and maybe even the denomination.

Waiting until an accident happens and claiming ignorance provides no defense against liability. Becoming informed and actively monitoring the safety of your church building and grounds is vital.

In this chapter we will look at disrepair and consider slips, trips, and falls. These constitute a large proportion of each year's claims. Weather and environmental issues are also of concern. Whatever the climate, weather can create a hazardous condition. Fire prevention will also be discussed. As I speak to leaders and pastors, I recognize that few have an adequate fire-escape plan. Finally, we will consider safety issues related to contractors and service companies.

Regular inspections by qualified persons and quick responses to hazards are critical to reduce the risk of injury, destruction of property, and loss of funds.

Disrepair and Slips, Trips, and Falls

Most congregations must rely on volunteers to do many tasks around the church. Without volunteer help, many jobs would not get done. As a result, many minor (and even major) repairs are often in the hands of a worker without the needed professional skills. Electrical, plumbing, and major repair work done by the wrong person can lead to more costly problems. One congregation that had several members who were handy with tools and repairs asked them to take a look at a malfunctioning church boiler motor. After numerous amateur attempts to repair the motor, professionals were called in. The job cost three times as much as it would have if professionals had been called in the first place.

With their own jobs, commitments, busy schedules, and other church functions, it is easy for volunteers to forget or postpone the task that needs to be done at the church. Most of us can think of at least one item in our church building that has been in disrepair for quite some time.

Often we ask people to do jobs that they don't want to do. I can't count the number of meetings I have attended where time was spent wrangling to persuade some member to commit to making a needed repair. Finally, to keep the meeting moving, someone will reluctantly say, "I guess I'll do it." Chances are that the volunteer isn't going to rush out and get the job done tomorrow. There is a good chance that the issue will be raised again at a future meeting.

Some churches have a thorough, regular inspection and maintenance schedule. But many do not. This gap may stem from the rotation of leadership, poor planning, and lack of a written policy. Ultimately, the buck never stops anywhere for long. As a result, inspections and repairs aren't carried out regularly. Some estimates say that nearly 55 percent of church claims involve slips, trips, and falls. Such accidents can easily be reduced by a regular inspection of the facilities and procedures for identifying and correcting problems.

At one church, during the fellowship hour for members and visitors after worship, a cup of punch was spilled—not an unusual mishap. Several members had seen the spill, but no one cleaned it up. A visitor slipped on the liquid, twisting her ankle. None of the embarrassed members bothered to contact her after the incident. Although she was not seriously injured, the woman never returned to the church.

This problem, which could have been much worse, points to a larger issue. People who visit our church expect that the congregation will take reasonable care for the safety of the facilities. Visitors do not expect to be injured while on our premises. Though we have insurance to cover such accidents, the burden of care rests mostly on the congregation.

Safety begins with the general upkeep of the property outside the building. Are the sidewalks uneven or cracked? Do we provide adequate lighting outside and in the stairwells? Is the playground equipment safe? Are there obvious hazards in the parking lots?

Inside, entryways should be clean, dry, and well lit. Adequate mats with beveled edges should be provided to absorb moisture. Stairways should have a slip-resistant surface. Any hazard should be marked immediately with orange cones and signs.

Inside the church we may find poor lighting, worn carpeting, uneven surfaces, poorly marked steps, loose handrails, inadequate housekeeping, slippery floor surfaces, spills or leaks, and equipment hazards—all with the potential of causing injury or loss.

Those in charge of maintenance and repair should constantly be on the lookout for things that need repair. A prioritized list of defects should be used to schedule repairs. If a repair can't be made immediately, the area should be marked or closed off, and adequate warning of the hazard should be given to all.

Even a spilled drink can cause injury. Train people to take the initiative and respond to even so minor a concern. Having someone stand by the hazard to warn others until someone can clean up the mess is a simple action that can prevent a fall.

Providing adequately supplied, clearly marked first-aid kits can also help, should there be an accident. Providing immediate aid to an injured person can make the difference between a minor and a major injury.

Finally, we need to be aware of the age and physical condition of the people we serve. Little children, the elderly, and the handicapped are especially dependent on us to keep the church safe. We all know that children can get into places that we would never imagine. Getting down to their level in the church will help us see otherwise invisible hazards. Keeping freezers and closets that contain hazards locked is critical. The elderly can experience problems with loose carpets, minor elevation changes in the floor, and dim lighting.

By conducting regular inspections, responding quickly to hazards, and maintaining general safety, a congregation can enjoy events with peace of mind.

Suggestions on Disrepair and Slips, Trips, and Falls

1. Ensure that lighting is adequate in parking lots, at entrances, and in stairwells.
2. Initiate a policy of regularly scheduled inspection and maintenance. At least twice a year conduct a complete top-to-bottom inspection. Beyond that, make frequent cursory inspections. Keep records.
3. Establish a quick, efficient system to repair hazards or mark them with hazard signs until repairs can be completed. Keep records of repairs.
4. Discuss floor coverings. Find the best procedure for safely mopping and waxing floors. Check carpets for unsafe conditions.
5. Determine who is responsible for attending to safety concerns any time the church building is used.
6. Make available sufficient mops, rags, buckets, and hazard signs to those who use the church. Mark the location of this equipment.
7. Use only qualified people to make repairs.
8. Make sure that adequately stocked and marked first-aid kits are available in key areas.
9. Consult your insurance company for printed or video materials they may supply to assist in reducing liability.
10. Always take extra care and concern for invited guests and other visitors.

Weather and Environmental Issues

Rain had been falling nonstop for three days. Many areas of town were flooded. Mr. England could hardly find a dry spot anywhere he went. Getting from his car to the church soaked him to the skin. As he entered the church, his glasses fogged up. Stepping forward, he slipped on water and fell, wrenching his back. Was the church responsible?

Depending on state laws, the congregation's liability for premises care may differ. In most states, congregations are usually not held liable when parking lots and other outside areas become suddenly hazardous with the onset of severe weather conditions. In other words, if obviously new ice and snow are on the roadway and someone gets out of his car in the church lot and falls, the church usually will not be held liable for injuries. However, if those staff or officers in charge of snow and ice removal were aware of the condition and did not take action in a reasonable time to correct the hazard, liability likely shifts to the church. What constitutes "reasonable" depends on the courts. If the pastor and other staff members came to the church and noticed the icy, slippery conditions and failed to have them corrected, and an hour later someone came to the church and was injured by falling on an icy sidewalk, the church would most likely be held responsible, since church officials were aware of the hazard and failed to respond in a timely manner.

Slush and rain can create a treacherous situation inside the church. Again, using the criteria of awareness and timeliness, the church would be held liable if leaders knew of a condition and failed to respond. Have a plan of action for responding adequately and quickly. Hazard signs, traffic cones, extra mats, and a mop and bucket would to most people indicate a hazard. If we intend that people use our church facilities, we need to take the lead in protecting them, and subsequently our congregation.

A more severe weather-related issue is the possibility that lightning could destroy your church. In fact, lightning strikes are the most frequent natural disaster. Though we may joke that the church is divinely protected from such occurrences, we know this is not true. Although no one is held responsible for a lightning strike, congregations may want to look into lightning-control systems and surge protectors for their equipment.

Common sense should prevail also in regard to environmental concerns. Some leaders may wonder if they could be held responsible for lead paint on chairs in children's rooms. We should realize that the question is not whether we are liable, but whether we intend to do the right thing and keep our children safe.

Lead paint, asbestos, and some of the chemicals found around churches may be hazardous to the health of members, visitors, and staff. We should look for ways to minimize use of such chemicals. Discard old, unused cans that contain known or unknown chemicals. Secure the remaining chemicals so that youth and children cannot get into them.

We should also take the initiative in asbestos removal, usually a costly undertaking. We should at least ask pertinent questions of our state or regional Environmental Protection Agency representatives about church buildings and risk. I found that representatives at the national EPA toll-free number are not prepared to address church-related asbestos issues. From what I did learn, up to four regulations apply to asbestos. Some apply to churches, but primarily in the renovation, demolition, or disturbance of existing structures. Before tackling major renovations or additions, it is best to check with a contractor and the EPA. Your state or regional EPA will send information to aid you in making correct decisions.

Weather and environmental concerns will probably not get a great deal of press anywhere. Most slips are not life-threatening. Nor is it likely that scores of people will drop dead of a hazardous chemical leak in our church building. This area is one where doing the right thing for people's health far outweighs the question of liability.

Suggestions on Weather and Environmental Concerns

1. Have a system in place for addressing hazardous conditions caused by weather. Know who is responsible at what times. For instance, does the snowplow driver come when you call or come automatically when two to four inches of snow have fallen? Are salt and cleanup materials readily available?
2. Make sure sufficient entrance mats are available.
3. Be prepared to place bright, large hazard signs in areas where they are needed.
4. Inspect your boiler and storage rooms for hazardous materials (cleaning agents, flammables, outdated substances, etc.). Discard all

materials that are not needed. Ventilate and lock up those you keep. Do not use your boiler room for storage.

5. Obtain information on asbestos from the EPA and determine whether a problem exists in your building.
6. Inspect painted chairs and painted surfaces, especially those accessible to children. If lead paint is found, take measures to correct the problem.

Fire Concerns

Worship had just begun in a large suburban church when the music was interrupted by the loud wail of the fire alarms. Stunned, everyone stood in confusion. Some moved toward the exits. Parents rushed for the nursery in panic. Some elderly people were afraid to move. The pastor was uncharacteristically speechless. Within minutes chaos was general. As it turned out, baked beans were burning on the kitchen stove. Someone nearby removed the smoking pan from the range and turned on a ventilation fan. The smoke had set off the alarms, causing massive confusion. Leaders of the church realized they did not have a plan for such emergencies.

In a far different setting, a small, rural church sat empty most of the week. There was no church office, and because of the small membership, few activities took place except on Sunday mornings. The church sat in a beautiful, isolated area. One night, the structure caught fire and, before anyone noticed, burned to the ground. The building, which had been the church home for many in the area for more than 100 years, was gone.

Michael L. Lindvall, in his book *The Good News from North Haven,* says of a church that burned down years ago, "Buying fire insurance for churches was seen by many in those days to be sure evidence of a weak faith. If you truly trusted that God would guard and prosper His church, the reasoning went, you didn't second-guess Providence by wasting money on insurance against 'acts of God.'"[1]

Although I hope that attitude is not the prevailing one today, some believe that the use of fire-detection equipment is a waste of money. But we need to know that arson is the leading cause of church fires. In 1994, 600 incendiary or suspicious fires in houses of worship were reported across America, with losses totaling about $16 million.[2] With the rash of fires in churches in the nineties, the Bureau of Alcohol, Tobacco, and Firearms has published a helpful "Church Threat Assessment Guide."[3]

Newer buildings are more often built with adequate smoke- and fire-detection equipment. Yet most older churches lack adequate detection systems. There may be fire alarms in your church, but if no one is there to hear them and they are not wired to a responding agency, what is their usefulness? It is also vital to have adequate fire-fighting equipment at hand. A small fire may be extinguished if a filled, working fire extinguisher is available nearby.

Most churches will not experience arson, but it is not uncommon to experience fire and losses caused by old, decayed wiring, inadequate equipment, poorly stored chemicals, or human error. Some municipalities and states have made it illegal to burn open candles at large indoor gatherings, such as a candlelight service. Though highly traditional and powerful, such events put the congregation at risk.

Some of our fire-prevention problems lie in poor education of the congregation, lack of explicit policies, inadequate or nonexistent inspections, and ignorance of fire codes. All can contribute to fires and possible loss of life and property. Training church leaders and members on the use of equipment, proper evacuation procedures, and posted emergency phone numbers should be a priority.

Suggestions for Fire Protection

1. Ensure that an adequate number of fire extinguishers, inspected annually, are placed throughout the building.
2. Train staff, leaders, teachers, and ushers in the use of fire equipment.
3. Ensure that clearly visible signs indicate the nearest exit.
4. Practice fire drills with your congregation, teachers, and leaders. Fire drills are a standard practice not only in schools but also in some commercial office buildings. Regular fire drills increase the possibility of order should there be an alarm or a fire.
5. Call in a qualified professional for periodic inspections of wiring and potentially unsafe areas and practices.
6. Consider installing a security/fire/sprinkler system wired to a 24-hour monitored alarm company.

7. As discussed in chapter two, consider a "church-watch" ministry.
8. Make sure you carry adequate insurance by evaluating it annually.
9. Ask the local fire department to:
   • Advise you of local and state fire codes and determine whether you comply with them.
   • Inspect exit doors for proper releases and exit lights.
   • Suggest improvements.
   • Become familiar with your building. One community required that a floor plan and access keys to every building be given to the fire department. Firefighters did walk-throughs to familiarize themselves with the building.
10. Make sure your church has a written policy on fire safety and procedures.

Contractors and Service Companies

The company hired to fix a light in the worship center was recommended by a member of the congregation. The member's brother owned the company and agreed to do the work for a fraction of what others would have charged. It was suggested that the labor might even be donated. The night after the crew completed the repair, a fire broke out at the church. The cause? Faulty wiring of the light. Who was responsible?

At another church, a company was hired to seal the roof. The first day on the job, one of the laborers fell off a ladder, seriously injuring his back. The church prayed for his recovery. Members were surprised to learn that the worker was suing the congregation for negligence. He sought the $1 million limit of the insurance policy. Win or lose, defending the claim would cost more than $100,000. Could the church be held responsible? Where would it get the money for a defense attorney?

As we all have observed, anyone can be sued, even a faith community. We live in a litigation-prone society. Explaining this trend, one attorney told me that the increase in the number of lawyers has forced them to look for new ways to earn their living. Suing religious organizations and other nonprofit groups is one of those ways.

The fact that a congregation has hired an outside contractor to repair, build, clear snow, or mow grass does not mean that the congregation has released itself from liability. These companies may expose your congregation to significant risk. Congregations need to concern themselves with the skill of those doing the work, the materials used, the supervision and safety measures in place, whether the work was subcontracted, whether releases were signed by all workers, and whether the company is bonded for accidents.

The first priority of the congregation is to protect its assets and people. To accomplish this aim, the burden of liability should be shifted to the contractor or company providing the service. By having a policy, asking the right questions, and obtaining written documentation from those who do the work, we can better protect ourselves from accidents and potential lawsuits.

In one case, even though the supervisor signed a "hold-harmless" agreement, an injured worker was able to collect from the congregation because he was unaware of the agreement. Every state views the law in its own way, and it is important to have these hold-harmless agreements in hand and ensure that those providing services are bonded. The wording of such an agreement should be viewed by the church's legal counsel.

Suggestions on Contractors and Service Companies

1. Check out the company by contacting churches and individuals who have used them. Ask if the work was done safely, in a timely manner, on budget, and as expected.
2. Try to have at least two companies bid on projects. Not only is this practice financially wise, it also ensures that you are quoted a fair price, and it could reduce accusations of an unfair bidding process.
3. Give all contractors and service companies a copy of your congregation's adopted policies for work done by such organizations.
4. Before any work is begun, meet with the contractor and address such issues as the skill of the work force, training, insurance coverage, length of the project, safeguards, hold-harmless agreements, and bonding of workers.
5. Especially on larger jobs, ensure that a contract is signed by all parties to cover general rules, fire safety, storage, protection, and other safety concerns.[4]
6. Appoint a person from the congregation to give general oversight to

the job. Have him ensure that all areas mentioned previously are in compliance.

7. If changes are needed during a job, get them in writing and have them signed by both parties. This precaution could prevent a lawsuit later over financial payment and added risk that may accompany the extra work.

8. Have your legal counsel advise you on forms, procedures, and contracts for working with outside contractors and service companies.

Stewards of Our Space

As one insurance brochure advises, "Being a good neighbor suggests you be open to helping people. Being a good steward suggests you take steps to avoid paying a claim arising from an activity not sponsored by your church."[5]

Although this statement refers to people who borrow or rent your facility, we can expand our thinking to all issues of building safety. Being a good steward means providing a safe environment for everyone who sets foot on church grounds. Not only do people need to know that we have provided the safest environment possible; we also want to be confident that we have done our best.

I am aware that few congregations can afford to pay for all the little jobs around the church. We simply must rely on volunteers. My suggestions are aimed at establishing continuity and ensuring that the right people do their jobs. Continuity and professional workmanship are not always easily achieved in congregational life. Therefore, we must work that much harder on these issues. Injuries and loss can have a lasting negative impact.

If we are building or expanding our facilities, the safety of workers and those using the premises during the construction phase should not be overlooked. And if our current building is showing signs of age, it is our responsibility to identify hazards, correct defects, and bring the structure and equipment up to a safe standard. Day-to-day minor problems need to be acted upon quickly.

The most logical way to carry out these building-safety procedures is to have a written and functioning policy. We need qualified, energetic people of initiative serving in leadership positions. The head of the trustee board and members of the congregational governing board should be self-starters who will set policy and follow through without extensive prompting and supervision. It is wise to get the most value possible from the congregation's dollar, but sometimes by pinching pennies, we compromise safety. Allocating adequate funds to get the work done and managing those funds wisely is also necessary.

One small, declining congregation had a large sum of money in its building fund. Although water poured in around the old, rotten church windows every time it rained, those in charge would not allow the money to be used for new windows. Apparently an unwritten but long-held rule specified that the fund could be used only for a *new* building project.

This anecdote is a sad commentary on the attitudes in many congregations. We often avoid writing down our rules and operating on schedules. We hate to offend people and therefore leave things undone. We trust the word of others and thus don't care much for written contracts. In the process, our building can become an unsafe place where people are put at risk.

By wrestling with these tough issues and trusting God in our struggle, we can become better stewards.

Questions for Self-Evaluation

1. Do we have policies for inspections, maintenance, and repairs?
2. Do our own members have the expertise to make repairs?
3. Do we have a list of qualified, bonded repair people at our disposal?
4. Are hazards visibly marked and corrected in a timely fashion?
5. Do we know who is responsible for general safety, oversight, and cleanup each time someone uses our facilities?
6. Do we have a policy to respond quickly to weather-related issues? What is our procedure for removal of ice and snow? Are messes inside the church cleaned up promptly? Do we make cleanup equipment and warning signs accessible?
7. Are our floor coverings safe? Are our stairwells in good repair and well-lit?
8. Do we have a printed, posted, and rehearsed fire-drill policy?
9. Would our members and visitors know what to do in case of an alarm or fire? Do we have special expectations of our leaders in such crises?
10. Do regular fire inspections take place?

11. Could we purchase a monitored security/fire/sprinkler system?
12. Are our fire extinguishers adequate? Are they inspected and filled annually?
13. Could we ask fire and insurance specialists to advise us on premises safety?
14. Do we traditionally ask for proof of insurance and written contracts on work to be done by outside contractors? Do we require signed hold-harmless agreements of all workers?
15. Do we check references of contractors? Do our by-laws require at least two bids? If so, do we follow that rule?
16. Are our own congregational officers bonded?
17. Is our insurance adequate to cover accidents and negligence?
18. Have we discussed contracts, coverage, and liability with our legal counsel and insurance company?

CHAPTER 4

Staff, Congregation, and Visitor Protection

On a routine day at a church in a midsized midwestern town the pastor and the secretary were going about their usual business when a man came in and asked to use the rest room. He was shown to the men's room and went in. Before anyone knew what was happening, the man came out and shot the secretary and the pastor. The secretary died of her injuries. The pastor survived the attack. When questioned later, the man told police that the gun had told him to shoot somebody. He was convicted and sentenced to prison. The families and the congregation were changed forever.

This sad account points to the perils we may face in our congregations. We should not assume that because we are doing God's work in God's house that nothing can happen to us. People do get hurt and killed in church buildings.

This chapter deals with crimes perpetrated in congregational settings. The victims and offenders are diverse. The first section deals with building access, focusing on how the people in our church may be exposed to dangers, and may thus become crime victims.

The victims are sometimes trusting and vulnerable children. These little ones and their families should feel safe when it comes to the care our congregation provides. Those who look to our congregation when they are weak and broken can also become targets of abuse. Fragile people, if not treated with loving care, can become victims at the hands of those in positions of power and control.

Youth can also be victimized. They are at a critical stage of life, developing physically, emotionally, and socially, and are prone to develop trusting relationships with those of either the opposite or the same sex. Youth workers, whether young or older, play a delicate role in

trying to promote positive development while keeping enough distance
to remain a friend and advisor. At times, the roles of both youth and
adult become blurred and may lead to unhealthy or illegal contact.

The elderly are not immune to becoming victims. Often having a
long history in the congregation, they trust the people at church and may
let their guard down. The offender may be a stranger who steals a purse
or someone known to members who takes advantage of the elderly.

Visitors, staff, volunteers, and members can all become victims of
crimes on church property. This wonderful place we call church may
feel safe to us, but trusting people and unsecured premises offer perpetrators an easy, undetected opportunity for crime. It's bad enough to
have our church broken into and items stolen. But it is truly horrifying
when people who use our building are robbed, injured, attacked, abused,
or killed.

We will also look at the importance of emergency procedures and
offer suggestions for avoiding unsafe transportation procedures. We will
then turn our attention to the care and counseling of our children, youth,
and adult members.

Admittedly, this chapter is graphic and may be seen by some as
alarmist. But unlike earlier chapters, which dealt with theft, break-ins,
slips, falls, and fire, this chapter deals with human loss. Crime victims
have had something personal taken from them. They became victims
where they thought it could never happen—in their church. Some have
done remarkably well, continuing to trust and serve God. Others, though
victimized many years ago, still bear open wounds and visible scars.
Theirs is a tattered trust.

As I listened to their stories, I realized that I did not want to water
down their truths. Some victims asked me to "get the story out" in a way
that might alert church leaders and thus spare other victims.

Some may think that taking steps to protect people in the church is
legalistic. They believe that God will protect them and that they shouldn't
tinker with that protection. But I believe protecting those who look to
our congregations for help, care, guidance, and nurture is not a sign that
God isn't doing the job. Ultimately, God is our shield, our strength, and
our stronghold. So we are urged to "Trust in the Lord, and do good; so
you will live in the land and enjoy security" (Ps. 37:3, NRSV). Events
are in God's hands. But failing to make plans for keeping human beings
safe in our congregations and on church grounds is equivalent to failing

to speak out on hunger, war, and injustice. (Some church members feel that those issues should not be talked about either.)

Parking Lots and Entrances

Choir practice usually ended around 9:00 P.M. each Wednesday. Mary, a choir member, left the building with other choir members. As they walked to the parking lot of the isolated church in this bedroom community, Mary realized that she had forgotten something and went back into the church. Returning to the lot, she went to her car. As she opened the door and slid in, she realized she was not alone. A man hiding in the back seat grabbed her. After the attack—she was raped and beaten—Mary crawled to the pastor's house at the other end of the parking lot to summon help. A suspect was caught, but because of technical errors in the investigation, he was never found guilty. Mary is still in counseling nine years later. The man is free; he still mockingly tries to make contact with her.

As a result of the attack, improved lighting was installed in the church parking lot. Many questions were raised. Awareness was heightened. Members were told to enter and exit the building in groups. No subsequent incidents were reported. But for Mary, these precautions came too late.

Even if we keep the interior of our church safe, we must not neglect the outside. Dark parking lots not only can cause injury; they can also leave people susceptible to a variety of crimes, ranging from robbery and car theft to rape and abduction. Why should a thief break into your car and hot-wire it when he has easy access to your car as you leave with the keys in your hand? Maybe the bad guy is not there to take your car. Many robbers will prey on women for their purses and on men for their wallets.

If car theft or robbery is not the criminal's objective, maybe it is rape or abduction. One 14-year-old in a small southern town told her parents she was going to the youth group meeting. They believed her. In fact, she walked across the church parking lot to a convenience store, where she willingly got into a car with three men, but was later forced to stay with them. She was released unharmed four days later. Her family, the congregation, and the community cycled through a wide range of emotions during that time and afterward.

Although this case wasn't one of outright abduction from the church lot, it points to the kinds of people who look for a chance to prey on our young. Instead of being safe at a youth group meeting, this girl found herself in a dangerous situation that could have turned deadly.

A dark or secluded lot is the sort of place that attracts people who seek to harm unsuspecting people. We do not want our members and visitors subjected to crimes. Nor do we want to experience guilt and shame as a congregation for not having taken steps to prevent a crime.

A spokesman for the congregation attended by the 14-year-old offered this summary of the issue of church security: "One thing we have known for a long time is that people come to church and they have the illusion of security."[1] The congregation responded by forming a task force to look at the entire church-security issue. Members envisioned a prototype model that would deal with all aspects of church security. The pastor said, "Churches and institutions should become more proactive in their philosophy, so they won't have to wait for a tragedy."[2]

Suggestions for Securing Parking Lots and Entrances

1. Install lighting that comes on automatically at dusk. Make sure all entrances and lots are well lit. Mercury lights offer the best illumination.
2. Light every entrance. There is a trade-off here. Do we spend money to keep the lights on all night, or do we ask the last one out to turn off the lights? All-night entrance lighting is an effective deterrent to break-ins, and it ensures that the last person out does not step into the dark.
3. Consider using lights on timers at entrances. If all meetings are normally finished before 11:00 P.M., set the lights to go off then. Be sure to adjust the timers for seasonal alterations of light and for the changes to and from daylight savings time.
4. Educate your congregation about arriving and leaving in groups. Choirs, women's groups, and those coming to evening meetings should be encouraged to practice safety in numbers. If they see a suspicious person nearby, they should return to the building and watch. If the person doesn't leave, the police should be called.
5. Trim the shrubbery around entrances. Thick, high bushes offer an

ideal hiding place. A criminal can lurk undetected behind dense foliage for a long time.

6. Ask a crime-prevention officer to speak to your congregational groups and advise you on security measures.

Weekday Access and Protecting Personnel

First Church has always been known for helping those in need. Its Samaritan fund provides money for meals, gas, and other essentials to the poor of the area. Most of the down-and-out people who come to the church know they can receive help several times a year.

John, one of the local poor, has been to the church often. He is believed by many to have a mental disorder. One day John arrived at the church and asked the secretary for help getting food. She informed him that the pastor was the only one who could sign the necessary form. John left.

In a short time he returned and asked to see the pastor. When the secretary told John the pastor was still not in, he began to yell and curse. He frightened her, threatening that if she didn't give him money, he would do something they would all regret. At that moment the pastor arrived, settled John down, and took care of matters. Later, John returned to apologize to the secretary.

As I did research for this guide, I walked into numerous churches and checked to see if they were safe and secure. At one church, I entered the unlocked front door and wandered around the church for five minutes, finding no one. There were no signs directing visitors to an office. I finally heard a noise and followed it. I found an office at the front of the sanctuary. I tried the door handle and was pleased to find that it was locked. But when I knocked, the secretary opened the door to greet a stranger who was now alone with her in the building. As we discussed her actions, the layout of the building, and my reason for coming, she admitted, as did many other secretaries, that she felt extremely vulnerable, especially when she was alone in the building.

The two types of people who may cause us the most problems during office hours are those who are mentally unstable and those who intend to rob us. Some mentally ill people may have problems with authority, the church, God, and everything that represents them. They may come to the church for a kind word or support. Or they may come to do harm. At an inner-city church a mentally ill man tried to enter a building that had a locked-door policy. Undeterred, he went up the street and stabbed a woman to death. Though shocked at the death, staff members realized that if the church had been unlocked, they could also have become victims.

Those who wish to rob people in the church are a brazen bunch. When I was a detective, a criminal once told me that churches, pastors, and religious people were to be avoided. In his mind, messing with God's people might bring the wrath of God upon him. But times have changed. The criminal mind is not something we will soon understand, but the previous "off-limits" sign apparently isn't as visible to today's criminals. They come looking for money, which they think churches may have. Many robberies and other crimes are perpetrated by drug users. In robbing us, a person desperate for drug money or high on drugs will not use good judgment in deciding whether to spare our lives.

In one large congregation in the South, the members strove to reach out to all levels of society in their ministries. In so doing, they hired a felon from a nearby halfway house as part of their maintenance crew. One evening, a female staff member was working late alone at the church. When she didn't arrive home, friends became suspicious. They went to the church, where they found her body. She had been robbed and strangled. Her killer was the recently hired maintenance worker, a felon with no violence on his record. The congregation responded quickly, and members came together in support of the family and friends. But they will never again feel the same about their safety in the church.

Although this would have been a difficult crime to prevent, we still need to make access to staff and members a bit more difficult. Installing several layers of defense is money well spent. We want a system that allows adequate access to members and friendly visitors that will also thwart those who have other plans. We must recognize, however, that there will always be an unavoidable tension between reaching out to others and keeping our members and employees safe.

Security alarms help prevent break-ins, but they can also serve as a first line of defense. Codes can be used to allow authorized people to let themselves in. Intercom systems will allow a staff person or volunteer to screen visitors before allowing access. Security cameras can help identify people in the building. Secure offices can protect staff from intruders.

Panic buttons can summon help. Most bad guys who see an elaborate security system will choose another location.

We have an obligation to provide a secure work environment for our staff and others in the building during the week. I realize that tension exists between trying to make everyone feel safe and continuing to be an open, accessible house of God. Finding the balance is difficult but not impossible. Doing so will allow those who use your church during the week to feel more safe and secure.

Suggestions to Ensure Weekday Access and to Protect Personnel

1. Consider using only one main door during weekday business hours.
2. Shop for a monitoring system (cameras with or without recording units).
3. Ask about the feasibility of a door-release system so that visitors must speak into an intercom and identify themselves before the door is unlocked by a staff person.
4. Consider placing an electric-beam system at the main door that signals when the beam is crossed by someone entering.
5. Equip the church office with a secure door. Consider a dutch door, so that the bottom door can be locked. Or have safety glass with a window and speaker hole, or a door with a remote release.
6. Discuss how to deal with emergencies. Consider an alarm-system feature that allows police to be notified in an emergency.
7. Discuss "code words" between staff members. Key words that alert others over the phone of a problem can allow a staff person to summon help or proceed with caution. Encourage secretaries never to tell outsiders that the pastor is gone but to say that he or she is unavailable. This ploy could lead intruders to believe that more than one person is in the building.
8. Train staff members and volunteers who come to the church during the week in emergency procedures. Practice these.
9. Tell staff to avoid agitating suspects or those engaged in a crime. Money and valuables can be replaced. Lives cannot.
10. Consider the balance between cost and safety. Find ways to improve the safety features you have now.

Emergency Procedures

The worship service was at its midpoint when a commotion erupted in
the choir loft. Choir members were jumping up and shouting for help.
Apparently something was wrong with the organist. No one was sure
what to do. Several people ran toward the organist. Others ran for help.
Some stood motionless. The organist, who had suffered a massive heart
attack, died later that day. No one had been trained in what to do in
such an emergency.

In another congregation, ushers noticed a suspicious man in the
hallway during the worship service. They began discussing what to do.
Several ushers went looking for the man. They noticed coats and purses
strewn on the floor. It looked as if there had been a robbery. The ushers
didn't have access to the telephone in a nearby office. One finally ran to
the basement phone and called the police. Hundreds of dollars in cash
were taken, along with several expensive coats. The suspect was never
caught. The ushers realized they didn't have a plan.

Incidents like these two happen in churches. We need to ask: Are
we ready for them? Possibly the most common emergencies in a congregation are health-related (heart attack, seizures, choking, injuries). Perhaps less common are brazen crimes (robbery, arson, attacks, kidnap-
ping).

In relation to health concerns, many practical measures can be taken
at minimal cost. Should someone suffer a heart attack or seizure, drop
over in worship, or begin choking at a congregational dinner, do you
have a plan? Some people, often those we least expect, respond instantly, offering immediate help. Others, who one might assume would take
control, freeze up or head in the opposite direction. We can't leave our
response to chance. Congregations need a clear, thought-out, written
process that is taught well and stated often. On a regular basis (at least
annually), emergency procedures should be practiced. What we practice
repeatedly will be our response in an emergency. Many people need to
know what to do if something happens in the church, because we never
quite know who will be there at a given time.

When it comes to bold crimes, many of the same principles apply.
It is unlikely that a given congregation will be robbed at gunpoint during
worship. However, such crimes do happen. More common is the sneaky
thief who wanders around the church, often posing as a lost visitor, looking for opportunities to steal.

Attacks and kidnappings in the church happen less frequently, though they are not unheard of. With these crimes, the primary concern is members' domestic problems—divorced or separated couples battling over child custody. It may be much easier for noncustodial parents to take their children from a church building than from a home. Nursery workers and teachers may release the child to the noncustodial parent, not knowing of the marital problems. Domestic violence has also taken place on church grounds.

A leader in a large California congregation told me that the church had armed, uniformed security for a short time. The feedback was negative. So a less invasive, low-key, plainclothes approach was adopted. Armed, radio-dispatched security staff still have the ability to respond quickly to any emergency, and yet few people are aware of their presence.

The church building is still a relatively safe place for most people. But we need to assure those who gather that they will be protected and that medical services will be readily available. The difference between an unplanned, chaotic response and a planned, rehearsed, and well-executed response may very well be the difference between life and death. Many people, after any incident, find themselves asking, "Was there something more we could have done?" Sometimes there was not. Yet how difficult it is to acknowledge that there may have been.

Suggestions on Preparing for an Emergency

1. Train as many members as possible (especially ushers) in cardiopulmonary resuscitation (CPR). Agencies will often come in and teach CPR classes at a reasonable cost.
2. For health issues, sit down with doctors, nurses, or medical providers to formulate a plan of action in case of a medical emergency. The plan should include:
   • Steps for notifying authorities
   • Location of stocked first-aid kits and oxygen tanks. (Always have these near heavily used areas such as the sanctuary and social hall.)
   • The names and locations of exits (northeast door, southwest door, etc.) to aid in telling the rescue squad or police which door to use.

- What you want others to do (call for help, leave the building, stay, pray).
- Posted and highly visible evacuation routes.
3. Train the ushers in the following:
   - How to detect highly suspicious people (a touchy issue). The key is not to invade a visitor's privacy. But introducing yourself, asking the person's name, and being alert are good methods not only for greeting, but also for thwarting an ill-intentioned plan.
   - Walking the halls during worship, looking into classrooms and securing doors.
   - Keeping their cool. It's a bad idea to try physically to stop a person from committing a crime. People get hurt. It is much better to get to a phone to alert police.
   - How to make an emergency call: Ensure that people know where an accessible telephone is located. State the emergency and location succinctly in a clear, calm voice to help speed the response time of the emergency provider. Give clear descriptions, direction of travel, and the assistance needed.
4. Alert teachers and nursery workers to be on the lookout for people who shouldn't be there.
5. Train teachers and volunteers on emergency procedures.
6. Educate parishioners on how to keep both personal and church valuables secure.

Transportation Issues

When I received a call telling me an accident had occurred involving one of our congregation's day-care employees and several children, a knot instantly formed in my stomach as I waited for the rest of the bad news. As it turned out, no one was killed. However, two of the children were in the hospital. We immediately assessed the level of the problem, notified parents, asked several day-care board members to come to the church to assist, and called our insurance company.

Fortunately, the injuries were not life-threatening. The children were released the same day, and we began assessing our transportation policy. As a result, we chose no longer to allow employees to transport children on field trips. Commercial carriers now do that.

In addition, our quick response proved effective. Our insurance company was immediately involved with the families. Even though the employee's insurance was the primary carrier, the families later remarked that the professional, prompt, and courteous way they were treated by our company's representative was highly appreciated. No lawsuits were filed.

Congregational transportation raises a wide range of concerns. Besides federal laws, each state has its own set of regulations. Many of these laws were passed after tragic accidents had taken many lives. Unfortunately, some of the worst accidents involved members of congregations.

The first area of concern deals with drivers. Each congregation needs to ask, "Who's driving the bus?" The two categories are those driving a congregation-owned vehicle (van, bus, or car) and those driving private vehicles to transport congregational members and friends. Federal laws prescribe who may drive congregation-owned vehicles. If a church vehicle carries 16 or more passengers or weighs over 10,000 pounds, the driver must have a commercial driver's license (CDL). In addition, drivers are required to undergo drug and alcohol testing.

It is wise to read the Federal Motor Carrier Safety regulations. The responsibility for compliance is with the congregation. You may contact your regional or state office of the U.S. Department of Transportation, Federal Highway Administration; write to the national agency at 400 Seventh St. SW, Washington, D.C. 20590; or call 202-366-4000.

Private vehicle drivers pose another concern. They are not regulated but can be held liable, along with the congregation. Having done youth work, I can tell you that I was happy when anyone stepped forward to drive. It didn't occur to me to check qualifications, license, and safety records.

Drivers are not the only safety factor. We should never transport people in anything but a safe vehicle. Congregations often buy older buses and vans, and it is important to keep them serviced and inspected. The inspection of vehicles and the accuracy of records may become issues in the event of an accident. Safety equipment should be kept on board.

Finally, responding quickly to an accident can forestall or reduce a lawsuit. Having a plan and implementing it quickly and caringly leaves a positive impact on people involved in a difficult situation.

Suggestions on Transportation

1. Screen every driver. Have written proof of insurance and driving
    record. Compile a list of potential drivers ahead of time. Ask the
    drivers to sign a form listing offenses, and obtain proof of insurance.
    Insurance companies will also conduct driver's checks. They take
    time but can be worth it. Also, most experts would agree, allowing
    youth to drive to events is a recipe for disaster.
2. Have a regular inspection policy. Besides regular, noted mainte-
    nance inspections, pre- and post-trip inspections are advised. Keep
    trip and inspection logs. Have someone qualified in vehicle safety
    to assist you. Inspections can also be conducted on privately owned
    vehicles.
3. Have a clear, written transportation policy that is shared with the
    congregation.
4. In congregation-owned vehicles, have fire and first-aid equipment
    on hand.
5. Instruct drivers what to do in case of an accident.
6. Require the use of seatbelts.
7. Use permission and release forms for trips.
8. Check your coverage with your insurance company.

Children and Youth

Possibly nothing tears at our hearts more than hearing of a child who
has been sexually violated. Accounts of such violations at the hands of
church workers and leaders are almost incomprehensible.

In a large congregation of 750 worshipers in the Midwest, the entire
children's program was growing rapidly. A weekday program that ministered to children of the church and community became increasingly
popular. The church scrambled to find older youth and adults to help
with the program. Two boys brought up in the church volunteered as
helpers. One day a child in the program let it be known that one of the
boys had touched her in inappropriate ways. Stunned at the accusation,
leaders called in the police to investigate.

Seven years later, many things had changed. First of all, the two
boys had been found guilty of numerous crimes and had served time. In

all, about 100 children were believed to have been violated in some way. In addition, accusations were made against others (adults and youth) in the congregation, including the suggestion of organized satanic activity. In all, lawsuits have totaled about $78 million. The church, now fractured, suffered a drop in worship attendance to 200. The four pastors departed, although some remained involved in litigation. The denomination provided support but seemed to distance itself from an active role to avoid legal implications. The saddest part is that the children have had to endure not only the trials and publicity but also the need for ongoing counseling and the probability of lifetime scars.

In retrospect it is clear that though program growth was favorable, safeguards were not in place to ensure children's safety. There were poor controls, record-keeping, supervision, and accountability as children moved from place to place in the church. Hundreds of lives were permanently affected.

In 1997, a Roman Catholic diocese in Texas was ordered to pay nearly $120 million to families and victims of child abuse stemming from misconduct at the hands of a priest.

In California in 1994, a Pentecostal pastor settled out of court for $1.75 million after five men accused him of sexually molesting them as youth.

The reports of sexual abuse in congregations are rising steadily. It isn't clear whether it is the incidents themselves or only the reporting of incidents that is on the increase. But it is clear that congregations are not immune from such incidents. The Sexual Abuse Information Page web site states that one in three females will be sexually abused before the age of 18, and approximately one in six males will be sexually abused before the age of 16.[3]

The major concern is the children who endure such treatment at the hands of people perceived to be people of God. Timothy Friend, a Christian private investigator and consultant on sexual abuse in congregations, states:

The most disturbing aspect of the problem is the devastation done to those victims who are harmed by sexual abuse. Whether the victim is a child or an adult, the wounds are deep and may take years to heal, if at all. Words cannot express the betrayal, spiritual confusion and pain felt when one is abused by a church leader. Victim support groups have formed because the congregation has often not been understanding or active in the healing process. Sexual abuse in the congregation has reached a crisis level and must be addressed.[4]

Besides the harm done to children and families, the impact on a congregation is huge. Friend says, "When sexual abuse does occur within a congregational setting, the subsequent problems are almost always devastating. Financial losses due to civil litigation as well as the loss of credibility in the community can cripple if not totally destroy a congregation."[5]

I would add that even unfounded accusations can cause enormous problems and divisions within congregations. Usually, after an allegation, human nature tends to "pick sides." We believe either the victim or the accused. The result can be feelings of betrayal and loss of trust. Many parents with children and youth are keenly aware of the frequency of reported abuse. These stories are often in the headlines. As they look for a church to join, parents are more apt to connect with a congregation that has a clear understanding of the issues of child and youth safety and that addresses them. Issues ranging from nursery security to supervision on a youth trip are important to parents.

Many good books and programs deal exclusively with this issue. It is possibly the most frequently addressed area of congregational security and safety. Some of the material comes in the form of checklists, while other complete programs offer handbooks, audits, sample policies, training options, response guidebooks, and release forms. Some of the resources are listed at the end of this book.

Reading these materials, I noticed that all seem to agree on basic guidelines we can adopt to keep our children and youth safer. In general, a written operating policy, screening, training, supervision, ongoing education, and a solid insurance policy are deemed essential.

These precious gifts to us—our children—deserve our protection, especially in the church. When policies are set and implemented, some members will become angry and uptight. Even when the faithful veteran who has been teaching church school for 30 years chooses to quit because of new policies, I encourage standing firm on the principle that protecting children is paramount in the life of the congregation. Do not compromise in this area. We must adopt procedures that protect the children, the congregation, and those who work with children. If we do, everybody wins, and God is glorified.

Suggestions on Children and Youth Protection

1. Have a complete written and posted policy on how children and youth are to be supervised and cared for.
2. When hiring personnel or looking for volunteers, make sure potential workers fill out an application with referrals. Check the referrals. Consider criminal background checks (some states require them). Congregations can be held liable for negligent hiring practices.
3. Consider a six-month or one-year waiting period before new members or attendees can be assigned to work with children and youth. This rule alone will discourage many pedophiles (those whose preferred sexual objects are children).
4. Consider adopting a rule that no adult may be alone with one child (except that child's parent). This "two-adult rule" should apply to both children and youth.
5. Supervise workers. Do spot checks and observe behavior and practices.
6. Have a plan for responding to an accusation. Don't hide it. Report any accusation as required and deal with it in a professional manner.
7. Train workers in emergency procedures.
8. Train workers about what is and is not appropriate touching.
9. Use a check-in/check-out system in your nursery and younger children's classrooms.
10. Discuss your congregation's policy and needs with your insurance agent. Make sure you have coverage for volunteer workers.
11. Use release and permission forms for outings and potentially high-risk events such as camping or hiking.
12. Purchase a child-protection program that addresses the safety of children and youth in depth, and implement it. Many companies and ministries are now offering tapes, classes, and workbooks on this topic (several are listed at the end of this book).
13. Consider starting a ministry in your church to care for those who have been crime victims in your community.

Counseling Concerns

Mrs. Jackson, a married mother of three, called the pastor and asked to see him about a personal problem. She indicated that she would be embarrassed to come to the church and wondered if he might come to her home during the day to counsel her. How should the pastor respond? He may be a good and faithful pastor who has a "go anywhere, anytime" attitude toward ministry. Or he may recognize the liability and temptation a home visit could present, cite the congregation's counseling policy, and politely encourage Mrs. Jackson to come to the office during regular business hours for counseling.

The world of the pastoral counselor is a difficult one. Trying to be trusting, available, and faithful while acting in a safe, wise, and responsible manner causes many pastors and lay counselors anxious moments.

Thomas Taylor, in his book *Seven Deadly Lawsuits: How Ministers Can Avoid Litigation and Regulation,* lists seven areas that get many pastors into difficult problems: fraud, defamation, child abuse, sexual misconduct, clergy malpractice, invasion of privacy, and undue influence.[6] Note that he doesn't mention bad preaching, poor administration, or inadequate evangelism. Those might get you fired, but the seven issues listed by Taylor could get you sued or indicted on criminal charges.

Complex issues are intertwined with the counseling process. First, temptation: Far too many pastors and lay workers have found themselves in situations that escalate into an involvement they never planned or intended. Before they know it, either by their own weakness or at the initiation of the counselee, physical contact is made, and the ethics of counseling have been breached.

Second, even if nothing happens, many pastors and church workers have found themselves unjustly accused of an inappropriate act and have realized that they have no defense, because safeguards were not in place.

Pastors and counselors also need to recognize their influence. Those who come to us for guidance often ascribe great authority to the clergy and other counselors. Some pastors and counselors use the power of their position to manipulate and violate a counselee.

Finally, even the "appearance of misconduct" is a concern. For instance, if a female pastor goes to a discreet location (restaurant, park, home) every Wednesday to counsel a married man, and people see them, questions and problems are likely to arise.

Much of this vulnerability goes with the territory of being a pastor or counselor. One should not become paranoid and avoid counseling altogether, but there is no point in being naïve about what can happen or appear to have happened.

Another counseling pitfall has to do with what the pastor says. What if, for instance, a pastor suggests during counseling that a couple stay together, even amid issues of domestic violence, and the women is then injured or killed at the hands of her husband? A pastor could be sued and lose the case.

Confidentiality in counseling can also become a legal issue. A pastor who used part of a counselee's story as a sermon illustration, without permission, betrayed confidentiality. Although the pastor believed that many people already knew the details of the parishioner's story, his failure to ask permission to share it resulted in embarrassment and anger for the counselee.

Finally, those who counsel minors need to be especially cautious. If a young girl asks to stay after youth group to talk, and the male youth pastor or youth director is alone with her, is there cause for concern? From a liability standpoint, the answer is a resounding "yes!" Again, even if nothing happens, the appearance, the temptation, and the lack of proper safeguards (the two-adult rule) could cause the young person, the adult, and the congregation a great deal of grief.

Doing ministry will always involve certain risks, because we are dealing with people. Counselors care for people in some of their darkest moments. Pastors and counselors should make every effort to keep themselves and their counselees safe at all times.

Suggestions on Counseling

1. Adopt and make known a written policy on who may counsel, when, where, and for how long. Recommendations on when to refer a counselee to a psychiatrist, psychologist, or psychiatric social worker should also be included. When a policy is in place, it can be referred to in a sticky situation. Train staff about these policies.
2. Always write your counseling appointments down on a calendar. Make notes of the session. Some counselors even tape conversations to protect themselves and then use the tapes for reference later.

Advise the counselee of such a policy before taping, and always secure all tapes of sessions.

3. Consider counseling only in your office and only during business hours. It is important that someone else know that you are there.
4. Make sure you carry adequate liability insurance for counseling.
5. For marital-conflict counseling, consider a capable mentor couple who could be trained and equipped to counsel together in a "para-ministry" with pastoral oversight.
6. Stay on your toes. Always ask yourself if a situation could be perceived wrongly and lead to an accusation. Also be aware of situations that might lead to temptation and an act of misconduct.
7. Train all counselors on proper abuse-reporting procedures, according to laws in your state.

The Cost of Safety

As congregational leaders and pastors, we have been called by God to care for those who are sent our way. To do so haphazardly or with malice is an offense against God.

Though we cannot protect all people, we can work on protecting those with whom we are involved in ministry. Well-thought-out, widely discussed and consistently implemented policies that keep people safe should be put in place in every congregation. Failure to have such policies in place may mean that members are endangered and may result in a significant judgment against the congregation and its officers.

Some people fail to see the need to spend money on insurance or to take the time and effort to set policies protecting against incidents that have never happened to them. Others believe it is wise to protect themselves against every possible occurrence. Any congregation that begins a discussion about insurance and security will meet with both support and significant resistance. Keeping people safe does carry a variety of costs. But a life may be saved because of our precautions. An injury or violation may be prevented. And even if we don't realize it now, the effort will have been worth it.

Questions for Self-Evaluation

1. Are our parking areas and entrances adequately lighted?
2. Are the entrances free of shrubbery and trees?
3. Have our members been taught safe ways to enter and exit the church building?
4. Do we have a policy for dealing with suspicious and dangerous people?
5. Are our entrances and offices secure during the daytime?
6. Have we asked our staff how safe they feel while engaged in ministry at the church?
7. Do we have a clearly written, posted, and rehearsed emergency plan?
8. Do we have a sufficient number of members trained in CPR?
9. Have we identified doctors and nurses in our congregation?
10. Are first-aid kits, phones, and oxygen marked and quickly available?
11. Have we trained ushers and other leaders in emergency procedures?
12. Do we ask all drivers to show driver's license, driving history, and proof of insurance?
13. Do we have a transportation policy?
14. Are all congregation-owned vehicles regularly inspected for safety? Are the inspections logged?
15. Are our policies and procedures on caring for children and youth clearly posted and understood?
16. Are we aware of laws on reporting abuse?
17. Do we have a specific hiring and supervision policy for staff and volunteer workers?
18. Do we have ongoing training programs for employees and volunteers?
19. Do we practice the two-adult rule?
20. Are we clear what steps we would take if an allegation were leveled against a worker?
21. Do we have a congregational policy on acceptable counseling procedures?
22. Is our insurance coverage adequate for the kind of counseling done by pastors or other counselors?
23. Do we have a sexual harassment policy? Is it posted?
24. Are all staff aware of what is appropriate and inappropriate touching?

CHAPTER 5

Hiring and Personnel

For months the congregation had sought a new youth worker. Leaders had checked with local colleges and seminaries. They advertised in the local newspaper and yet received only a few inquiries. The youth group was dwindling, and help was needed. Then an acquaintance of a member stepped forward: A nice looking young man, he had just completed his service in the Air Force. Speaking to the pastor, he told how he had accepted Christ two years previously, while in the service. Since his discharge, he hadn't found a church and would like to be considered for the job. He planned eventually to go to Bible college.

The applicant was introduced to several of the church leaders one Sunday after worship. A few questions were asked, and the young man was hired. He seemed to have energy and a sense of discipline. The youth seemed to like him, and the youth group grew over the next few months. Many thanked God for sending this young man—that is, until detectives arrested him, just four months after he took the job. He was charged with the rape of a 14-year-old girl from the youth group.

An investigation showed that sex-related charges had earlier been filed against him in the service. His discharge was less than honorable. The young girl had told a friend about the rape, and the friend had told her parents. The victim entered therapy, and her family sued the congregation for negligence in hiring practices. The congregation lost the case.

Much of this chapter covers standard personnel issues. Taken separately, each step is routine. But together, they can enable your congregation to establish a pattern of screening and selection that will better assure the safety and security of members and help prevent your congregation from being sued by either a victim or a disgruntled worker.

According to James Cobble, publisher of *Church Law and Tax*

Report, "More than 60 percent of lawsuits are resolved for between $100,000 and $150,000. However, the average total cost, when legal expenses and other costs are taken into account, is $1 million."[1]

This chapter deals with the selection of both paid and volunteer workers. Many congregations jump for joy when a volunteer steps up or when a high-quality candidate applies for a job. We want to believe that these are good, faithful people, seeking to do God's work in a congregational setting. Most of them are. The vast majority work out to our satisfaction. They may stay for years. But regardless of our track record, serious consideration should be paid to hiring and selection policies. Though employees and volunteers are often treated differently in congregations, many of the same issues arise in hiring and selecting both. Most congregations take a serious look at a prospective staff member. Volunteers, on the other hand, are often welcomed without much thought. Seldom is there an application form or interview. If a pedophile (someone with an unnatural attraction to minors) could volunteer to work with youth with no screening, isn't it logical that he or she would do so?

The process I recommend includes steps for advertising a position, accepting applications, and interviewing and screening applicants. Also advised is the creation of an employee manual to make clear what we expect of the staff member.

A well-written job description provides a benchmark to evaluate whether workers are completing the job satisfactorily. If they are, you may want to promote them or increase their compensation. If they are not, you may attempt to correct the problem or seek to terminate their services. The importance of written evaluations will be discussed, as will appropriate ways to terminate an employee.

Carrying out these supervisory responsibilities correctly will minimize the risk of safety and security problems arising from the poor selection and oversight of paid and volunteer workers.

I was surprised when the administrator of a large church with more than 100 employees told me that it had no overall policy for selection or hiring. The process was left to the head of each department. No documentation of an interview was required. Background checks were conducted only for certain jobs and not in the hiring or selection of youth and children's workers.

Many churches hire only one or two people every year or so. It is understandable that they have no firm policy in place. But whether one employee is hired or 100, congregations need a policy. Without solid, practical guidelines, we leave the process to chance. And by doing so, we may open the door to potential problems that could exact a steep price.

Paid Staff

Let's walk through the process of hiring a worker for a paid position. (Many of the principles apply to volunteers as well.) Although this chapter is not meant to be a comprehensive guide to hiring procedures, it is important to view each step from a security and safety standpoint.

First, a position should be advertised. You may advertise in your congregation and others, including congregations of other denominations. The point is to find someone with a knowledge of congregational operations and a faith in God. If you run ads in the local newspaper, you will probably draw a wider variety of people, some of whom have no religious background.

Job candidates should complete an application form. This form is the first step to understanding as much about the applicant as possible. Note that some questions are illegal on job applications. Generally, questions about gender, age, religious beliefs, and physical disabilities are forbidden under federal civil rights law and the Americans with Disabilities Act. However, sometimes a church may in fact be allowed to discriminate on the basis of religious practice. The grounds for doing so are complex. Suffice it to say that a policy must be in place and in practice prior to the employee selection process. Some states have laws that make it impossible for congregations to discriminate on virtually any grounds.

You may be able to ask about criminal offenses, charges filed or pending, misconduct, use of alcohol and drugs, traffic offenses, work history, and references. However, it is likely that questions about lawsuits and judgments against former employers may not be allowed. It is wise to have legal counsel review your application and selection process before you put it into operation.

Applications may also provide the applicant with information. Informing applicants that you will be seeking their permission to conduct a criminal, employment, and financial check and will be checking references may cause candidates with a troubled past to think twice about applying. This does not mean that people who have had problems should be excluded from applying for a job or being hired. The application process seeks to obtain truthful and accurate information. These first steps will help put the applicant on notice that your congregation is serious and thorough in its selection of employees.

Applicants should receive a written job description. You can use that document later as a guide to performance standards. Again, safety and security are enhanced. The job description informs applicants of the guidelines for the job and appropriate employee behavior. It also helps protect the congregation from lawsuits for wrongful termination. For instance, if you have a written two-adult rule for working with children, and you find that the employee is not adhering to it, he or she cannot claim ignorance of the policy.

The job interview is best conducted by a team consisting of pastor and church leaders rather than by an individual, so that reactions and observations can be shared. Begin the interview by introducing the candidate and seeking to put him or her at ease. Ask clear questions related to the application and the job. Again, certain questions are allowed and disallowed in each state. Ask your legal counsel about laws in your state to protect your congregation from accusations of hiring discrimination. Some people have great credentials but a questionable work history. The interview should be a time to probe for issues that may not be readily clear on the application. Uncovering a problem in the interview could save your congregation from later grief.

After the interview, the team should feel free to compare notes and to raise concerns. Any perceived problem should be discussed openly. Again, if these concerns blossom into a problem later on, it could become necessary to terminate the person, and the damage done may be impossible to correct.

Once the most likely candidate is selected, a further screening process takes place. Depending on the position, you may wish to do a criminal, employment, driving, or financial check. Advise the applicant that you routinely do such checks, and secure a signed release form from the candidate authorizing them. These checks will cost money, but they often point to concerns not discovered in the interview. I would also urge the checking of references. Some applicants list names to impress the employer. Follow through, and if questions arise, keep digging. Being safety- and security-conscious in hiring may seem tedious, but the benefits are worth the effort.

If a person checks out and is selected, have an employment form signed that clearly states the job description, salary, vacation benefits, and any other pertinent employment information. Some congregations use an employee manual that contains everything from job descriptions to salary, benefits, and other important personnel issues.

After the new employee begins work, it is wise to have regular evaluations. Turning employees loose to find their own way can lead to unacceptable behavior and work habits. If their bad habits later result in a legal proceeding, the courts will look at what care and supervision your congregation provided. You may choose to do a ninety-day, six-month, and one-year evaluation the first year, and an annual evaluation thereafter. Good evaluations depend on adequate supervision.

Following the entire process from advertising to evaluation is necessary to assure your congregation that they are attracting, hiring, and maintaining employees that practice safe and secure work habits. Workers should have not only the congregation's safety in mind; you need assurance that they make the security and care of children a high priority. Although you can help people with unsavory pasts, you do not want thieves, sex offenders, or chemically dependent people involved in the day-to-day operation of your facility and programs.

One denominational publication notes, "As other professional children and youth-serving programs and agencies implement more effective screening techniques, church programs will be an attraction to chronic child abusers."[2] If we are not aggressive and professional in our hiring practices, this laxity will become known to possible offenders, and we may suffer the consequences.

Suggestions for Hiring Procedures

1. Advertise in those places where you will attract people with the qualities you seek.
2. Review your application form. Is it complete and legal?
3. Provide a pre-interview session for your interview team. Discuss goals and review applications. Ask how the process relates to security and safety.
4. Conduct a fair, legal, and thorough interview. Engage the applicant

in talking about work history and life experience beyond the standard questions on the application. Look for indications of character.

5. Screen the applicant further. Consider criminal background checks (required in some states for certain jobs), employment, and financial checks. Make sure the applicant signs a release.
6. Check references. If a concern arises, check further. Answer any lingering questions.
7. When an employee is hired, immediately issue an employee manual that includes all aspects of employment. Have the employee sign that he or she has read and understands it.
8. Supervise and evaluate the employee. Document your evaluations and positive and negative feedback from others.

Volunteers

In many congregations, the selection process and supervision of volunteers are far less rigorous than they are for employees. But when we consider the risk to people in our congregations, volunteers usually have wider access to children and members. Nearly every faith community has a much larger number of volunteers than employees. There are notable differences between the employee and the volunteer, but the application, interview, screening, supervision, and evaluation process should be similar.

Not many congregations ask volunteers to fill out an application. They believe the volunteer would find this request offensive and invasive. Most congregations are glad enough to have anyone volunteer, and assume that if the volunteer is made to jump through too many hoops, he or she won't be interested in the task. Once a volunteer is selected, many of us expect that the person will remain in the position until he or she drops over or moves away. We often don't set a clear term of service for the position.

The other school of thinking argues that the more we legitimize the position, the higher quality of volunteer we will attract, and the safer and more secure we will be. I doubt that many thoughtful church leaders would say, "Those few people we hire who deal with programs and administration should be of high quality, but the volunteers who more often deal with children, youth, and money should not be screened." I have spoken to leaders of several congregations that have moved from a casual approach for recruiting volunteers to a more professional process. Few made the transition without some groaning—and even all-out battles. Some longtime church-school teachers quit. And yet the congregations held to the principle that they desired the best, most qualified people involved in their ministries. The leaders realized that the well-being of all members was more important than the personalities of a few.

I recommend easing into a new process of requiring volunteers to apply, interview, and be screened and evaluated. Begin by educating the congregation on the importance of high-quality ministry. Ask for feedback, hold discussions, and phase the program in over a year or two. Although some members may fight it all the way, many will agree that the new process is a better way to go. The real beneficiaries will be those who are served.

The key to any good volunteer program is a high-quality person (possibly paid) who will oversee the recruitment and adequate supervision of volunteers from beginning to end. Supervision and evaluation should be ongoing. Developing the forms and conducting the checks can be time-consuming. Correcting problems along the way can be exhausting. You may be lucky enough to have a qualified volunteer to take on this task. But a personnel manager, coordinator of volunteers, associate pastor, or other paid employee is a key ingredient in maintaining a well-designed and implemented volunteer corps.

Volunteers are an important part of congregational life. Whether they work with children or do a menial cleaning job around the church, a congregation should desire the best effort possible from volunteers. Helping volunteers expand their abilities will, in the long run, promote an attitude of doing the best for all of God's people. Our job as leaders is to identify the gifts of people and place them in ministries and opportunities that God has suited them for, and then help them grow in those ministries.

Suggestions for Dealing with Volunteers

1. Begin discussion and education about liability issues in regard to volunteers.
2. Consider phasing in a program of selection and training over a year or two that includes measures to enhance security and safety.

3. Include in the process an application form, interview, evaluation, and supervision.
4. Consider using a one-year covenant for volunteers. Evaluate them on performance and commitment as well as on how well they follow safety and security measures.
5. Designate a coordinator to be responsible for volunteers.
6. Continue to train volunteers in their area of service. This activity keeps motivation up and problems down.
7. Inform all volunteers in their training of their legal responsibility to report incidents of misconduct.

Job Descriptions and Employee Manuals

When I became pastor at my present church, the music director, who does an excellent job, told me that he had worked for seven pastors over 30-plus years. I would be the last pastor he would work for, he added. He was, at some point, going to retire. I thanked him for telling me, invited him to stay as long as he felt comfortable doing the job, and asked him to let me know ahead of time when he planned to leave.

The model employed by some congregations would be to wait until the director gives a two-week or one-month notice and then begin looking for a replacement. I've used this method often. But this time I'm trying to stay ahead of the curve. I've begun working with the music director on an accurate job description. I want to know exactly what he does. Although not every congregation would choose this approach, I have asked him to be part of the process of selecting the right candidate for the job. I would like to hire the new director before our present director leaves. With his wealth of knowledge, he would be the ideal person to mentor the new director for a short time.

People in all positions have the potential to put your congregation at risk. If an employee is not selected, oriented, and supervised with care, his or her actions could lead to lawsuits and grief within the church. We are looking not just at dollars and cents, but also at the credibility of our congregation in the community.

Clear, accurate, and current written job descriptions and employee manuals can alleviate many headaches. Consider a situation in which an employee quits without giving notice. If you have a clear position description, you can move ahead immediately in filling the job. If not, you

may have to settle for an interim period when someone not fully qualified fills the job and places the congregation at risk. When you hire a
candidate to replace an employee, you should be able to say from the
beginning, "Here is what we expect of you." The job description leaves
little to the imagination, and evaluations can be based on it.

Employee manuals should include a job description; a signed employment agreement with starting date, salary, and pay periods (weekly,
bi-monthly, monthly); sick, personal, and vacation policies; and an explanation of benefits (health, insurance, allowances). The manual should
also make clear how and when evaluations will take place, how employees are to be supervised, and when opportunities for pay raises will come.
Include in the manual information about congregational or denominational policies, procedures for handling reprimands, grounds for termination, reporting of misconduct, a sexual ethics policy, and any other responsibilities. By including these elements in the employee manual, a
congregation lays a firm foundation for evaluating and, if need be, ter-
minating an employee. In regard to safety, security, and legal exposure,
these steps help close up many issues often litigated.

The employee should be required to read and sign the manual and
job description. The congregation can often protect itself and its employees by getting the employment contract in writing. Verbal communication will seldom be seen as binding in a court of law. In addition,
changes of pastors and other leadership take place. Signed and dated
policies can continue through these changes.

Suggestions for an Employee Manual

1. Have a manual for every employee.
2. Keep it updated, with the most current date noted.
3. Include in the manual job descriptions, hire dates, vacations, salary,
    and policies on any personnel issues that could arise in a dispute.
4. Make sure the employee reads and signs a statement that he or she
    has read and understood the policies and procedures.
5. Forward all changes to all employees for inclusion in their copy of
    the manual. Have them initial a sheet to show that they received the
    changes.
6. Hold annual meetings to educate employees on various provisions in
    the manual.

Evaluations

A laywoman in charge of personnel issues for her congregation called and told me a story of an employee who had not worked out. The man had violated many provisions of his job description and of the employee manual. The laywoman wondered how best to dismiss the employee. I asked if evaluations had been regular. They had not. Was there any written documentation in the employee's file indicating problems? Had the employee signed an agreement stating that he understood and would follow the guidelines in the employee manual? Again, the answer was no. With that, I told the caller that she might be hard-pressed to terminate the employee. Unless laws have been broken or flagrant behavior is detected, a fired employee may have grounds to appeal the dismissal and put the church at financial risk.

I recommend establishing a 60- or 90-day probationary period for new employees. This time allows all parties to decide if the employment decision was a good one. In most states either party can opt out with good cause. In some states, no cause is needed. Sometimes the decision is mutual. Even if things are going well, a written evaluation at this time is valuable. The simplest procedure is to have a discussion with the employee, see how things are going, and identify areas of concern or positive aspects of his or her performance. Write up a brief summary and have each party sign it. Give the employee a copy.

Conducting an evaluation again at six months and at one year gives you a minimum of three entries on the worker's performance. If at any point you have reason to discuss performance, positive or negative, with the employee, a notation should be made. Any warnings, spoken or written, should be documented in the employee's file. Should there be letters, positive comments, awards, or achievements, they should also be added to the file. These files should be locked up for security.

Especially in congregational life we should look for positive things to say about our staff. In the congregations we serve, we should give people the benefit of the doubt on most issues. When people do God's work well, they should be well compensated or affirmed in other ways. And when they do a so-so job, we need to encourage and help them to do better. If they do poor work and put the congregation in peril or at risk, we are responsible to make the necessary changes to restore credibility to that area of ministry.

Some people appear to think that God's work can be done haphazardly or sloppily, and that God and others will nonetheless be pleased. To the contrary, I believe that even though God does not ask us to be perfect, we need to ensure that we offer God and the family of God our very best. When that doesn't happen, and when people are exposed to unnecessary peril, we need to have documentation on hand to support making a change.

Suggestions for Evaluation

1. Devise a standard evaluation form. Keep it simple.
2. Attempt to set a professional but relaxed atmosphere when conducting an evaluation session.
3. Agree in advance on the areas to be evaluated. Some employers choose a few areas from the job description as the focus of an evaluation, instead of trying to cover all areas in one sitting.
4. Allow the employee to do some self-evaluation. Employees often point to areas of which you were unaware or mention concerns you have before you bring them up. Discuss safety and security measures related to the person's job.
5. Document all evaluations and discussions about performance.

Termination

For a long time, an employee in a congregation I served had not been performing to the leadership's satisfaction. We worked with her, made suggestions, and notified her in writing of performance standards. After my departure, the congregation terminated her. Several months later, the congregation received notice of a complaint filed against them by the former employee, charging wrongful termination. The congregation's attorney wrote a letter indicating the reason for her dismissal and citing the documentation on hand to justify the termination. No further action was taken on her part.

I wish all terminations went so smoothly. Some dismissed employees will seek revenge or take legal action. Others will fight back, sometimes physically. Terminations are no fun, but it is important that we prepare for them, have proper documentation, carry them out with precision, take measures to protect ourselves from assault, and do whatever is necessary to follow through.

Soon after I arrived to serve one congregation, it became evident that our day-care director was not meeting our needs. When we discussed the issues that troubled us, the director gave us conflicting stories. Finally we decided to dismiss her. We had adequate documentation from performance evaluations, as well as letters and proof of flagrant violations on her part. I asked the director to meet with two congregational officers and me in my office at the end of the day. We confronted her with the concerns, pointed to the previous written warnings, affirmed her in several areas, and then asked her to resign. We offered to pay her two weeks' salary if she would resign on the spot. She cried and expressed remorse. We told her that she could come the next morning to collect her belongings. She left the building, and we felt that we had done a good job. Unfortunately, we had neglected one important safeguard.

In our attempt to be as kind as possible in a difficult situation, we were naïve. Sometime during the night, she came to the church and removed the majority of the files from her office and several other items she claimed were hers. She took records on children, other employees, and day-care evaluations and procedures. It took us months to regain control of the day-care center and bring our procedures into compliance. We also changed the locks to the church. By our incomplete planning, we exposed the congregation and our day-care operation to unnecessary risk while we sought to recover from her actions.

Though we did a few things rights, I have learned better ways to terminate an employee. I would still choose to take the high road, showing as much respect and care for the person as possible. It is up to the employee to choose whether to receive this respect. I would have adequate documentation, as we did. Having one or two others present was a wise precaution to prevent inaccurate allegations later. Some leaders advise the employee that the meeting is being recorded to ensure accuracy.

But the preferred way to terminate an employee is to meet with your advisors and devise a strategy. Pray about the process from beginning to end. Once you choose to confront the person, it is important that you control the agenda. The employee may resign quietly or may try to negotiate another chance. He or she may become angry and lash out. I advise against getting into a debate or shouting match. Should the meeting escalate into a potential physical confrontation, don't become a party to it. Stay in control. If your calm manner fails to quiet things down, call the police. Your primary task is to state the facts, allow the employee to respond, and conclude the work needed to facilitate an acceptable parting.

If the employee will listen, discuss the conditions of termination. First, ask for all keys to the building. Next, if possible, offer two weeks' or a month's pay, on the condition that the employee leave without creating a conflict. Inform him that he is not to return to the building unless you are notified first. Pay him only if he complies with the negotiated agreement, which you ask him to sign. Failure to meet conditions of the agreement will mean forfeiture of further pay. Whether or not a separation agreement is signed, the person should be escorted to collect personal belongings, then taken to the door. Advise him that you will keep him in your prayers and follow through with the promise.

Once the former employee is gone, notify other employees of the action and what you expect as their response. Advise employees what information should not be shared and what additional work they will need to do because of the loss of an employee.

This procedure may sound cold and less than godly. However, though we have an obligation to each person, we have a larger obligation to the entire congregation. Protecting members and their families and congregational assets is also our duty. Some for-profit corporations have personnel departments with specialists known as "terminators," whose job it is to dismiss employees swiftly and mechanically. Doing so in a religious setting goes against our instincts, as it should. But sometimes we are called to do the work that few wish to do. And when we do it, we should do it right, while at the same time keeping those involved safe.

One final note: Some behavior that we might consider poor performance may be rooted in a deeper personal problem in the employee's life. Before we are too swift to terminate, we should discuss with the employee what is going on in her personal life that may affect job performance. If the employee confides in you and shares a problem, offer to assist her in finding help. Some congregations will grant a paid leave of absence to those needing to sort things out. The congregation may also pay for counseling. Handling such a leave in a discreet manner is not easy, but if the employee is able to make adjustments and correct problems, she can often be restored as a positive, valuable team member. She will, one hopes, appreciate your concern and effort.

Suggestions for Terminating an Employee

1. Document all problems with employee performance. Make sure you have grounds to terminate. Consult legal counsel if necessary.
2. Pray about how to carry out the termination. Formulate a plan and involve one or two others in the meeting.
3. Stick to the facts and stay focused on the agenda.
4. Keep everyone as safe as possible during this tense time.
5. Attempt to negotiate a fair separation agreement. Ask the employee to sign it.
6. Escort the employee to his or her work area to collect belongings and then to the exit door.
7. Make sure the dismissed employee hands over all church keys.
8. Follow up by notifying other employees immediately. Answer any questions you can without breaching confidentiality.
9. Notify the congregation, again without divulging details.
10. Continue to pray for the former employee.

Stewards in the "People Business"

It makes sense to do a good job in hiring and selecting paid workers and volunteers. The problem is that many church members don't want to involve themselves in the hassle of change. Nor do many want to be "the heavy" who suggests and administers the changes necessary to ensure sound safety and security procedures involving personnel. This reluctance is understandable. Change is difficult in congregational life. Change that could affect the lives of many is downright scary.

But a shift in our thinking is necessary to prevent our congregation from becoming the place of operation for a pedophile, thief, deviant, reckless or drunk driver, or otherwise dangerous employee or volunteer. Once again we must weigh the costs—including the cost of doing ministry for years to come in our congregational setting.

Gladly, we are in the people business. We minister to people. We rely on people to make ministry happen. We need to do whatever we can to make the work environment in our congregation a pleasant, wholesome, and secure one. We have an opportunity to make the church a great place to work—and thus reduce the possibility of problems caused by employees.

To select, screen, train, supervise, and equip the people of faith well is profoundly faithful. To do otherwise is to practice poor stewardship of resources. If this area is left to chance, it will catch up with us. By the time we recognize that we haven't done our job, it may be too late.

Including a section on hiring and personnel in your congregational security and safety policy will minimize the chances of a dangerous or tragic incident. Besides reducing your risk, it will ensure a longer, more fruitful ministry to your congregation and the world.

Questions for Self-Evaluation

1. Do we have job descriptions for all positions? Are they current? Do they carry the date of the most recent revision?
2. Is our application form complete? Does it meet legal requirements?
3. Do we have a plan for the interview process? Do we know what questions to ask?
4. How do we screen and check an applicant's background? Do we conduct criminal, employment, or financial checks? Do we check references completely? Does the applicant sign a release permitting the checks?
5. Do new employees sign an employment agreement?
6. Do we have an employee manual? Does each employee get one?
7. Do we conduct regular evaluations? Is an evaluation report put in writing and signed?
8. Do we have a plan for termination? Is termination carried out in the presence of a witness?
9. Do we collect the keys immediately after a person is terminated?
10. Should we offer a separation package in a way that will help reduce the risk of loss or legal complications at the hands of the terminated employee?
11. Have we evaluated whether the employee's unsatisfactory performance is due to a personal problem that may be corrected?

12. Do we have specific performance criteria for volunteers? Should they complete an application form? Are volunteers screened, supervised, and evaluated?
13. Is a staff member or lay volunteer specifically responsible for coordinating the work of hired personnel and volunteers?
14. Have we begun discussing the importance of hiring, volunteer, and personnel policies?
15. Have all our policies been reviewed by legal counsel to reduce legal exposure?

CHAPTER 6

Criminal and Civil Liability, Insurance, and Other Issues

The phone call to the chair of the administrative board sent his head spinning. The pastor had called to let him know that the administrative board, the congregation, the pastor, and the individual board members were all being sued. "Can they do that, Pastor?" asked the board member. "I guess they already have," the pastor replied.

Thus began an ordeal for the congregation that lasted several years, cost over half a million dollars, and caused massive loss of income, members, and standing in the community—all this for a lawsuit that could have been prevented.

With more frequency, congregations are being sued. What can be done to protect and insure your congregation? The idea is to minimize risk, and if a horrible incident occurs, try to control the damage.

This chapter outlines who may be held responsible or liable. Can plaintiffs sue only the church? Can they also sue individuals? Are the officers of the congregation liable or responsible for the actions of others? Can a plaintiff collect even if a congregational officer was unaware of the incident? What happens when a suit is filed over an incident that happened a decade or even two decades ago?

We will discuss training for boards, officers, and staff. By offering such orientation and training, a church may reduce its liability. It is critical that church officers know what they are saying yes to when they agree to serve on the board.

Another topic is legal representation. Statistics have shown and my discussions with congregational leaders bear out the fact that many congregations do not have legal counsel. Many wait until the need arises and then look for an attorney. Some legal organizations are beginning to specialize in legal practices involving churches. Having an attorney who understands the dynamics of church law and organization can be an asset.

We will also discuss insurance. Does your congregation have the right kind of coverage? Is it sufficient? What exactly does it cover? What is excluded? How can you tell if an insurance company understands congregations? Several good insurance companies specialize in insuring churches.

If the worst happens and your church is sued, will your congregation be prepared? James Cobble, founder and executive director of Christian Ministry Resources, says that his research indicates that 1 in 50 churches will be sued each year, with the number one category of claim stemming from an injury.[1] If there are accusations, an investigation, charges, a claim, or a lawsuit, will you know how to respond to questions? A prompt, professional response to the alleged victim and the family can often reduce the risk of a lawsuit. How will you notify the congregation of an incident? How much should you tell members?

When a newspaper reporter calls or a TV reporter shows up with a camera crew, who will speak for your congregation? What should and shouldn't be said? Can you prevent staff and members from talking to the media? A comment to the media may surface later in a trial. Care should be taken to avoid further litigation for slander or defamation of character.

Finally, we will concern ourselves with the question, "Should we as a congregation press criminal charges or sue an offender?" Whether the offender is part of our congregation or from outside, we have several issues to consider.

All of these items are important. They deal with the "what if." We will discuss steps that need to be put in place "just in case." If there is no plan and people are uninformed, the most likely result is chaos. And even the smallest incident may be compounded if the proper response is not forthcoming.

Liability and Responsibility

The Rev. Thomas Taylor, a pastor and former attorney, says we are in an age of "litigation overkill." A minister's worst nightmare, he says, is "a large group of lawyers gathered to discuss the best way to sue clergy and churches." In fact, the American Bar Association did just that in 1992, when it offered a seminar on the topic.[2]

The object of a lawsuit is to collect money from any party that can be identified as having knowledge, oversight, reasonable suspicion, or direct or indirect control, or that can be linked in any way to an incident. That pretty well includes almost anyone—pastors, officers, staff, volunteers, denominations, and middle-judicatory officials. Not only can you be sued if you knew about a situation or incident and failed to respond in an appropriate and timely manner, but you can be sued even if you *should* have had reasonable knowledge and didn't.

Anyone can be sued. Litigation has become an American habit. We hear about seemingly ridiculous lawsuits and wonder how they could have been filed and collected on. After his divorce, one man sued his congregation, seeking to recover his contributions. He alleged that the pastor had failed to perform his counseling duties. The man and his wife had sought counseling from the pastor for conflict in their marriage. When the marriage ended, the man felt he should be able to recover the money he had given as his regular pledge to the church.

People who formerly would never have considered suing a congregation are seeking legal advice on far-fetched claims. If it's possible to collect, a plaintiff will pursue the case.

Who is liable in our congregations? Virtually everyone can be. And it is important to let the staff and congregation know that. Serving as a volunteer or a paid staff member carries responsibility. I have asked my staff members always to ask themselves, "Does what I am planning have the potential to get me or the congregation in a bind?" I urge them not to get paranoid and uptight about the issue but always to have it in mind.

When planning a "lock-in" or trip for the youth group, the youth director should be thinking about injury, supervision, youth-to-adult ratios, safe transportation, and release and authorization-to-treat forms for medical emergencies. To the horror of one congregation, two youth group members slipped off during a retreat and engaged in sex. The girl became pregnant, and although no lawsuit was filed, people wondered what quality of supervision was in place. The youth director didn't stay very long after the incident. Another youth pastor took a group to summer camp. When they returned, all of the seventh-grade boys had pierced ears and earrings. The youth pastor had suggested it. He didn't finish out the week in his position.

When anyone is involved in an official capacity in an activity under the authority and knowledge of the congregation or its leaders, the congregation may be found liable. When a volunteer congregational officer, conducting business related to her position, is involved in an accident in her own vehicle, she can be sued. But the church may also be held liable, as the officer was acting as an agent for the church.

Congregations may be held liable for actions that happened years ago. A common example is a case of sexual misconduct. An adult enters counseling and in the course of treatment realizes that he was violated many years ago as a youth. The case becomes public, and often others step forward to say they too were victims. The pastor or church worker who is the target of the investigation may be long gone from the congregation. The church officers of that era are now off the board, deceased, or living elsewhere. Nonetheless, the congregation is sued and found liable for failing to provide oversight and safety.

Simply stated, any ministry of a congregation involves risk and potential liability. Accepting this fact and preparing for it will lower stress and anxiety. Taking steps to prevent risks by advising and educating workers and providing continual oversight can help to minimize risks and liability. Responding to a potential or actual incident and having sufficient insurance are also crucial.

Suggestions Related to Liability and Responsibility

1. Educate staff and officers on the risks associated with their positions. An attorney familiar with church law would be a good choice to conduct this training.
2. Let volunteers know that their actions could cause the congregation to be held liable.
3. Conduct random checks of congregational functions and assess whether the risk is high or low.
4. Communicate with congregation members about their role in reducing risks in their church activities.
5. Post instructions and procedures (location of exits, use of kitchen and other equipment, location of safety equipment, procedures in case of an accident) in visible places.

Training

In my own denomination, all pastors of my regional conference are required to receive training about sexual misconduct. Documentation of
attendance is placed in each pastor's personnel file. We are also expected to post a sexual-harassment policy in a visible location in the
church. The training is helpful, sensitizing us to a wide range of issues.

On the horizon is a training session geared toward protecting children in our congregations. A task force has been working for several
years to put together a conference policy that will not leave the protection of children up to the individual congregation. It will involve training and oversight at the conference level. Training will be provided for
pastors and congregational leaders.

I'm glad to see this commitment to training and equipping our leaders and congregations. But the training also helps the conference limit
its own liability—not a bad thing. Judicatory and denominational leaders recognize that they are often included in lawsuits in these delicate
areas. The reason? From a legal perspective, their role is to provide training and oversight. If they do not train and oversee congregations, they
are, depending on the denominational structure, responsible for the lack
of training and thus the inappropriate actions of their pastors.

Levels of the denominational hierarchy are sued because of their
"deep pockets." If I am trying to collect for wrongdoing inflicted upon
me by someone in a congregation, how much will I get? Maybe not much.
But if it can be shown that this incident occurred because of poor training and oversight on the part of the denomination, then I have gained
access to a much larger pot of money.

The same principle applies locally. If a congregational volunteer or
employee is found negligent or guilty of a crime, there is a strong possibility that the officers and pastors will be included in a lawsuit—not
only as a group but as individuals. Those who sue may have access to
members' personal funds if it can be proven that the members were
somehow at fault.

Training can significantly reduce the chances that individuals will
be held liable. Board officers, staff members, and others engaged in
ministry should have proper orientation, training, and ongoing education. They should be clearly advised of their potential liability. It is
unfair and less than honest not to let congregational officers know what
they are saying yes to when they agree to serve.

I have been surprised by the degree to which the awareness level and commitment to make necessary changes rise when congregational leaders are informed that they can be held personally liable for their actions or failure to act.

The best time to train is when annual changes in leadership take place. Reserving an entire meeting for training can provide a valuable experience. Put all necessary documentation into leaders' hands. Policies, employee manuals, minutes of past meetings, financial information, job descriptions, and a chart of congregational structure should all be included. Saying, "Just come on board, and we'll tell you what you need to know as we go," is a prescription for disaster. After the training, officers and staff should sign a document attesting that they have received the training and understand its contents.

Help leaders to understand that attendance at meetings, especially policy-setting meetings, is imperative. Attendance shows that the leader cares about the business of the congregation. Lack of attendance may imply negligence of duties. (Even if a board member was not present at a particular meeting, he may still be held liable as a member of the board.)

Board members, other lay leaders, and pastors are responsible for policy and oversight of the functioning of the congregation. Ensuring that they are oriented, trained, and equipped will go far to lower their own liability as well as that of the congregation.

Suggestions for Officer Liability Training

1. Set an annual date for orientation and training of new officers.
2. Compile a handbook containing all necessary documentation.
3. Obtain a signed notice that each officer has read and understood the manual and his or her job description.
4. As part of ongoing training, brainstorm with the board on ways to reduce risk in your church.
5. Consider designating a congregational officer whose job description includes liability and risk reduction.

Legal Help

"Isn't it nice to have an attorney join our church? Now we can have him represent and advise us on legal matters." I heard this comment in a church, and I winced. I am glad that a lawyer joined the church, but to assume that the congregation's legal concerns are over is far from accurate.

If you have lawyers in your congregation, consider using them at least for advice. You may receive their services for free or for minimal fees. Yet recognize that they may not handle the particular areas of law that you need. Most good lawyers can advise on simple legal matters. They are able to file papers, review legal documents, and give general advice, but may not be qualified to handle an investigation, jury trial, or other litigation. Just as we would not ask a foot doctor to operate on our heart, we may not want to ask an insurance company attorney to advise us in criminal proceedings. Usually she will tell you if a matter is beyond her area of expertise.

If you are accused of a crime or are the target of a lawsuit, you want the best representation available. That's why it is important to establish a relationship with an attorney now. Sadly, many churches wait until the bad news arrives before seeking a competent attorney. Whether the attorney should share your faith tradition is up to the congregation to decide. There are several keys to the selection of legal counsel. First, the attorney should be accessible. If your attorney lives in another state or county and works for a large firm that handles many clients, sometimes access is a problem. Most congregations need legal counsel on mundane, daily issues, and don't want to wait forever for a response.

Next, the lawyer selected should be knowledgeable and effective in church matters. I have had my income-tax returns prepared by well-respected tax people. All were nice people who appeared to know what they were talking about. However, I found out twice the hard way that many aspects of clergy income taxes are unique. Once I ended up paying much more than I should have. Another time I got a second opinion and saved myself about $2,000 in taxes. Not all lawyers know church law. Actually, few do. So it is important that you choose as your attorney someone well versed in state and federal law as it pertains to the church, as well as in the constitution and canon law of your own denomination.

Finally, the cost should be clear. Find out up front what having an attorney will cost your congregation. Ask for a fee schedule. Hire a reputable lawyer whose fees are within your budget.

Organizations are springing up around the country that deal not only with defending the congregation when something bad happens but also with training and prevention in relation to security and liability issues. You may also find help on the Internet, in religious magazines, or even in the Yellow Pages. There are also organizations for Christian attorneys. (One such group is noted in the list of resources at the end of the book.)

Instead of using the attorney who represents the congregation, the pastor and leaders may choose to have personal attorneys. Especially in litigation between two parties in the congregation, a conflict of interest may arise between leader and members.

The key to this matter, as one attorney told me, is to "have a lawyer in your pocket." It is certainly in everyone's best interest to have a relationship with legal counsel before help is needed. You may or may not have to pay a retainer. Some lawyers will accept you as a client knowing that they will receive compensation as you use their services.

Suggestions on Legal Counsel

1. Identify lawyers in your congregation and ask them for some initial direction about finding legal help.
2. Interview lawyers and understand their mindset, qualifications, understanding of church law, and potential conflicts of interest.
3. Select an attorney who can assist in simple as well as complicated legal matters. Sometimes a firm can provide these services when an individual may not be able to.
4. Ask for a fee schedule. Understand ahead of time what an attorney will cost your congregation.
5. Set aside congregational funds for legal matters.
6. Educate your attorney on congregational policies, bylaws, and structures, and be open to legal advice on areas in need of change.

Insurance

The pastor becomes angry with a parishioner who challenges his authority. He punches the member in the face. Could the church be held liable? Does it have insurance coverage?

The financial secretary embezzles thousands of dollars over a period of years. Can the congregation recover the loss through insurance?

The outreach dinner coordinator runs across town to pick up day-old pastries from the supermarket. On the way back, she hits a child crossing the street. Could the church be found liable?

Church insurance coverage is designed to protect the congregation, its leaders, and its staff from suffering a huge loss. The insurer considers all possibilities that could put the congregation in peril and seeks to provide coverage.

Some of us see insurance as a necessary evil. We cringe when we write the check for it. We sometimes question whether we really need it. We wonder if those people writing books and manuals and leading seminars on church security and safety are alarmists. We realize we've had insurance forever and have paid in much more than the company has been asked to pay out.

That's the nature of insurance. We hope never to need it, but when we do, we hope we have enough to cover our losses. The variety of companies and types of coverage can make choosing insurance a complicated matter for congregational leaders. Most companies boast that theirs is the best coverage. Some say they offer the best service. How should you decide?

Though the details are hard to sort out, we can start with some common denominators. Deciding what company or agent to work with is the first priority. Don't just open the phone book, close your eyes, and point. Consider that most insurance agents fall into two categories: "independent" and "captive." The independent works primarily for the client, your congregation. The captive works for the company. Some congregations may choose to work with an independent who will find them the best rate. Other congregations may prefer to find the best company and use one of its local agents

The company you select may be highly respected in the field. Most companies could provide adequate coverage, but several specialize in providing appropriate liability insurance coverage for congregations. The service they render to congregations is normally excellent. They process claims quickly and efficiently, and they offer materials to assist in reducing risk. The key is finding an agent and company that will become a partner with you.

Ask about the types and amount of coverage needed. I find that most companies recommend the same coverage, but they use different names or lump specific coverage options into various categories. They may list five, six, or eight categories. One denominational publication clearly lists the areas of needed liability coverage:[3]

1. Commercial general
2. Pastoral professional
3. Directors' and officers'
4. Employment practices
5. Owned automobile
6. Hired and nonowned automobile
7. Umbrella
8. Pastor's personal

Check with your insurer and ask what coverage you have in each of these areas.

The commercial general liability coverage is the basic portion of your policy. It covers injury, property damage, personal liability, and employee-benefits liability. The pastoral professional insurance covers the pastor while he or she is acting in the official capacity of pastor. Experts overwhelmingly recommend directors' and officers' coverage. One company defines directors and officers as "all persons who were, now are, or shall be directors, officers, trustees, or members of an official board of governors, including elected or appointed church boards, councils, or a similar governing body while acting within the scope of his/her duties as such."[4] This coverage will protect your directors and officers from being held personally liable as a result of acting in an official capacity.

Employment-practices insurance protects the decisions you make on personnel. This insurance covers such matters as improper termination, unsafe working conditions, and sexual harassment. Owned-automobile coverage is necessary when the congregation owns a vehicle. Purchasing the expanded auto coverage means that privately owned vehicles will also be covered, should the auto owners' own coverage not be adequate.

The umbrella coverage includes the add-ons necessary should the basic policy be deemed inadequate. Also, should excessive claims be made in one year, this umbrella would help. Finally, the pastor's personal liability covers such things as an accident in which a guest is injured at the pastor's privately owned home. The pastor can be covered under the congregation's policy, but a special rider is necessary.

In addition to the eight areas listed, congregations may want to consider worker's compensation protection, employee-theft coverage, dishonesty and fidelity bonding, replacement-cost coverage, volunteer-labor protection, special building-project coverage, and special weather-related coverage unique to your geographic area.

There is some difference of opinion, but most insurance companies suggest no less than $1 million in general liability coverage and $2 million aggregate coverage. It is critical to look at all options, select the company that will give you good service, compare prices, and purchase the coverage that will best serve your congregation.

Suggestions on Insurance

1. Review your policy every year. See whether it covers the areas listed here. If not, consider adding necessary protection.
2. Contact your insurance carrier when the congregation adds equipment, personnel, or programs. If special projects are planned, check to see if volunteers are covered.
3. Videotape an inventory of your church. Include all areas inside and out. Note valuables. Make copies of the tape and lock them in a safe place, away from the church.
4. Keep a written inventory of valuables and equipment. Note the date of purchase and purchase price, and keep a file of warranty information.
5. Consider doing comparison shopping every few years with your insurance policy.
6. Ask your denomination for information. I have been amazed at what a denominational agency will send upon request. (It is too bad that some denominations wait until congregations ask.)

Responding to an Investigation or Lawsuit

It's 6:00 P. M. and you, the pastor, just sat down to supper. The doorbell rings, and as you answer the door you see two men in business suits on your porch. They show their badges and identify themselves as detectives with the local police department. You invite them in, and they begin asking questions about a person in your congregation. Before long, you realize that they are asking personal questions about you and that person. Though you have not yet been accused, their investigation obviously involves you. How far are you obligated to cooperate with their questioning?

As a former police officer and now a pastor, I believe we should do whatever we can to respond politely and refrain from interfering with any police investigation. When one is innocent of a crime, it would seem to make sense to cooperate with authorities quickly to clear one's name. Even if you are not accused and are asked simply to give a statement, should you be willing? Maybe not.

To help us to answer that question, let's look at the job of each of those involved. The job of the investigator is to collect evidence and statements and seek to uncover the truth in the case. Each detective or uniformed officer comes to the job with areas of expertise as well as with certain prejudices. As a detective, I often felt the pressure to find the guilty party, wrap up a case, and bring the criminal to justice in a timely manner. The vast majority of detectives are highly competent, but even the sharpest investigators will admit that they sometimes suspect the wrong person. In addition, their zeal can cause them to press too hard on people involved in the case. Mistakes do happen in investigations.

Next, consider the pastor's job as leader of the congregation. Pastors should have the best interests of the people of God in mind. They should also show care for any accused person or accuser. They should be truth-tellers. They should never bear false witness. Yet even the most godly person can get caught up in the rapid-fire questions of an investigator and give answers that could be taken in ways other than intended. Sometimes this happens without the pastor's even knowing it.

If the pastor is the one accused, telling the truth may be difficult, especially if he or she is guilty. Many people involved in illegal and immoral behavior live a life of lies and cover-ups. But the innocent person

accused can also get tangled up in an investigation that takes a long
time to unravel. Sometimes the damage done can't be repaired. The life
of a falsely accused pastor, church worker, or volunteer can be destroyed by misplaced words and erroneous statements.

With all of this in mind, I still recommend cooperating as fully as
possible with investigators. However, though my former colleagues in
law enforcement may disagree, if there comes a point when you believe
you are being accused, if you are charged, or if someone in your congregation is being investigated, consulting a qualified attorney is in your
best interest.

When a lawsuit is filed against the congregation, a member, or a
staff person, an insurance investigator may call on you and ask you to
answer questions. As above, be polite, but when the questions are of a
nature that may tend to implicate you, call your attorney.

Sometimes you will be surprised when papers are served. Process
servers love to serve subpoenas in creative ways. They may do it during
a meeting, in the church parking lot, or even during worship. These
papers will compel you to appear at a hearing or deposition to answer
questions in connection with a lawsuit. You may be the accused party or
a person who has the information sought.

It is important to call your attorney and discuss your obligations and
your approach to the lawsuit. Many cases never get to court. They are
settled before trial. One note regarding congregations: Any settlements
using church funds may be challenged by members. There have been
cases in which members, as donors, challenged a settlement, contending
that they had not authorized the funds they gave to be used in such a
way. Always check with church bylaws and legal counsel before agree-
ing to a settlement.

How we respond to any accusation, investigation, charge, or lawsuit
can make a large difference in the outcome. One church had a clear plan
and responded to an accusation and a subsequent charge of misconduct
on the part of a youth worker by offering the victims and families immediate care and counseling. No lawsuits were filed. Our appropriate response and dignified conduct are crucial.

As leaders and workers in the congregation, we are speaking not
only for ourselves. When we speak, we represent the people of God. We
have a responsibility to speak clearly, honestly, and carefully when talking about those with whom we do ministry. Making reckless statements

about anyone at any time can do harm. We should seek to embrace Matthew 10:16: "[B]e as shrewd as snakes and innocent as doves" (NIV).

Suggestions on Investigations

1. Have a qualified attorney "in your pocket."
2. Consider written procedures that will guide your response, should an investigation occur.
3. When visited by an investigator, show courtesy, listen, and consult an attorney if any accusations are made.
4. Consider training leaders, staff, and directors on how to handle an investigation.
5. Don't be afraid to ask questions of investigators. Their job is to get answers by keeping you off guard. Stay in control.
6. Don't panic. People really are presumed innocent until proven guilty. An investigation doesn't always mean that a person is guilty. A derogatory statement, especially about a falsely accused person, can later be used against you in a civil proceeding.

Public Comments

The secretary of your congregation receives a call from the local newspaper asking her to verify that the pastor is under investigation in an abuse case. What should she say?

The youth pastor is contacted at her home after a fatal car accident involving one of the youth on the way home from a church-sponsored ski trip. Should she comment?

A member entering the church building is approached by an investigative reporter from a local television station who wants to ask questions about the custodian recently hired by the congregation. Should he refer the reporter to an appropriate spokesperson?

Who speaks for your congregation? Is there someone clearly identified as the spokesperson? Can the comments of your members, staff, or leaders cause serious harm? Shouldn't everyone have the right to speak his mind?

While this is a free country and people should feel free to speak openly, comments made to private investigators, newspapers, and TV reporters can cause serious harm to a congregation and its people. If, for instance, the secretary had not heard the news of an investigation, she would obviously be rattled by the call. Any responses she made would be spoken out of shock and disbelief. Her comment, never intended to be "on the record," might be quoted on the evening news or in the morning papers. Such comments could compound the problem and cause deep embarrassment for those involved.

In the case of the fatal car crash, what if the youth director said, "I didn't even know that one of the youth had driven for the ski trip"? It seems an honest and innocent response, but in the hands of a plaintiff's attorney or a jury, her comments could be construed to mean that the youth director did not give reasonable oversight to such outings. That interpretation could weigh heavily in a later lawsuit or court case.

It is wise to inform the staff and congregation that they are not to make comments without first checking with someone in authority (the pastor or the board chair). It is wise to designate a person ahead of time to serve as the "official spokesperson" for your congregation. Comments to press or media may be made by that person only.

It is more difficult to guard against an unscripted comment by a member of the congregation. Good reporters use the advantage of surprise and shock to get information from people. They want impulsive, spontaneous answers. They are looking for a revealing sound bite or piece of information to use in an investigative story. The best you can do is to notify the congregation as quickly as possible and ask that members not make statements to the media. It will be up to them to honor that request.

In my experience, media and private investigators use every advantage *you allow them.* And that's the key. You have a right to create reasonable boundaries. Sometimes this boundary-setting gets touchy. One congregation had to enter into hasty and serious negotiations with the media and check its legal rights when media crews tried to enter the church to film the funeral of a police officer.

Let those in your congregation know that they have a responsibility to treat others as they would like to be treated. Making comments without accurate information can cause emotional harm and strained relationships.

Suggestions on Public Comments

1. Designate an official spokesperson for your congregation. It is wise to have a capable backup ready in case the spokesperson is unavailable or involved in the incident that has prompted questions.
2. In case of an incident likely to spark publicity, gather leaders and develop a unified, written response.
3. Inform leaders, staff, and members that they have the right and should exercise the right to make no comment until all facts are gathered.
4. Notify the congregation of a major incident as soon as possible so that members are not blindsided by reports and inquiries. Encourage them to use restraint in their comments.
5. Inform legal counsel as soon as you are made aware of a major incident.
6. Notify denominational authorities and your insurance company as necessary.

To Prosecute or Sue

Bob is a young man who has been in and out of trouble since childhood. The congregation has helped him find a job, given him groceries, and offered him guidance. Bob has helped do odd jobs around the church for pay. He has, on occasion, attended worship. After a series of break-ins at the church, police inform you that they have arrested Bob for the crimes. Should you press charges?

I have been asked by several people to advise them on whether it is appropriate for a congregation to press criminal charges or sue an offender. This area is a difficult one. Each case must be judged on its own merits.

Perhaps Bob, when confronted, is deeply remorseful, asks for forgiveness, and agrees to pay back the several hundred dollars taken. Because your congregation has a history with this young man, it may be a perfect opportunity to show him firsthand what forgiveness and grace are all about.

But maybe he is defiant, refuses to accept responsibility, and challenges you to press charges. It may be in his best interest to experience the criminal justice system. You still can connect and offer prayers and help, but within the system.

The Word of God is clear about dealing with those who have wronged you. Go to them and try to reconcile. Offer the olive branch. If they refuse, take another person with you. The objective? To give them every opportunity to make things right.

If the offender has no connection to the congregation, and he is given a chance to admit guilt and does not, then again, prosecution may be acceptable. You have a responsibility not only to your congregation, but to others in society as well. Putting someone on the street who is a habitual criminal may not be in the public interest.

Suppose the offender is from within your congregation. What about the embezzler or thief? What if abuse is involved? Again, each case must be decided on its own merits. If there is remorse and a chance for recovery and rehabilitation, the church can sometimes take on that role. At least the pastor can refer the person for help.

But in the case of sexual or physical abuse, the possibilities narrow. Sometimes there is no other option than to let charges be filed. State and federal law will not allow perpetrators of some types of crimes to go unpunished. As a congregational leader, you may be breaking the law if you fail to report some crimes.

If you decide to sue an offending party, be cautious. Prayer should be part of your response. A congregation and its leaders should seriously question their own motives for action. If their motives are to inflict punishment or to make themselves feel better, then the action may be misguided. Some might like to retaliate for having been deceived, when in fact their own carelessness and lack of planning allowed the incident to happen.

I have seen congregations offer an amazing quantity of grace. Sometimes it pays off, at other times it backfires. I have also seen congregations press criminal charges or sue. Members often experience a greater sense of grief than expected. They think they will feel better once the offender is put away or is made to pay. Seldom do they.

In some cases another option exists. In a growing trend, church people with legal conflicts are entering into mediated resolution rather than litigation. These ministries bring two parties together (families, church members, employees, and even offenders and victims). The idea is to help the parties hear each other clearly and work out a solid, mutually agreeable plan for resolving the conflict. It is a healthy alternative to the legal system.

Thank God for the ability that is given us to acquire wisdom as we go. We don't have to have all the answers ahead of time. Many times, in the midst of troubles, God will show us the way to go. Probably no decision about whether to press charges or sue will please everyone. But the One we should seek to please first is God. Take these things to the Lord in prayer. A crisis can become a transforming time in the life of the congregation.

Suggestions for Dealing with Crimes and Offenders

1. Consider the history the congregation may have with the offender.
2. Ask if there are mitigating circumstances.
3. Try to determine if the offender feels remorse.
4. Decide if restitution is possible. Usually while a person is in jail, making reparation to those harmed is not possible.
5. Determine if there is a chance for rehabilitation of the offender.
6. Try to determine the motives of the congregation.
7. Consider contacting a conflict-resolution specialist.
8. Seek wisdom and guidance in prayer.
9. Once a decision is made, leave it in God's hands, yet continue to offer care and concern to the offender.

Asking the Right Questions

The bad news is, whatever we do to protect outselves, our congregations may get sued or embroiled in an ugly investigation. But the good news is, the more we do to take the initiative in recognizing and limiting our congregation's liability, the less likely we are to be a part of such a traumatic occurance. The key is asking as many as possible of the questions listed in this book and acting on the answers. Please recognize, a list of concerns for congregational safety and security could be endless. Virtually everything we do could cause us to lose sleep and expose us to liability. Many knowledgeable people and organizations have spent years identifying specific areas and training congregations in those matters.

They include

- Tax issues
- How we elect or select congregational leaders
- What we do about legal documents
- Records and minutes from meetings
- Specific payroll issues
- Managing congregational day-care and school facilities
- Complying with copyright law

I urge congregational leaders to seek information on these issues, which go beyond the scope of this guide.

In covering what I believe to be the key areas of concern primarily related to the church building and the people within it, my purpose is to encourage congregations to begin discussing and asking questions about congregational security and safety.

Questions for Self-Evaluation

1. Does our congregation have ways to evaluate liability?
2. Do we conduct orientation and ongoing training on liability for our officers and leaders?
3. Should we consider having a congregational safety officer who deals with liability and risk?
4. Do we have a designated legal counsel for our congregation? Does our attorney know church law? Is the firm or attorney affordable and accessible?
5. Do we conduct an annual evaluation of our insurance policy?
6. When adding new programs or staff or engaging in a potentially risky activity, do we verify coverage with our insurance company?
7. Do we carry at least the minimum coverage on the eight areas mentioned in this chapter? Does our congregation have other specific coverage?
8. Do we have a current, accurate, written or videotaped inventory of valuables and belongings?
9. Is there a written policy on how staff, leaders, and congregation should respond to an investigation or lawsuit?

10. Does our congregation have a designated spokesperson?
11. What procedures will we follow in case of an incident?
12. Who will determine if we should press charges or sue?

Isaiah said, "The wolf will dwell with the lamb" (Isa. 11:6, NAS). We have all seen examples of bitter adversaries becoming loving friends. The love of God can do powerful things. Some day, I believe, Isaiah's prophecy will come to pass. But for today, good and evil are waging battles. Against and within the family of God, the storms of life are raging with increased intensity.

As I conclude this book, it is hurricane season. The first two big storms just hit Texas and the East Coast. The news reports have been filled with stories of how people approach the impending storms. Some homeowners and vacationers pack up and go as soon as it looks as though the storm could hit their area. Others wait and watch, preparing their homes and families. They keep a close eye on the path of the storm. Sometimes the hurricane will veer away at the last moment and spare them any major damage. At other times they will feel the full force of the storm. Some of those who have waited and watched will scatter at the last minute and head inland. Some batten down the hatches and stay, no matter what. Others even have a hurricane party, thumbing their nose at Mother Nature.

Our varied reactions to congregational security and safety are similar. The storm warnings are here. If you haven't experienced a storm in your congregation, thank God. But throughout this book I have offered real stories of people and congregations that have been beaten down by storms. Some have been able to rebuild; others are forever shattered. They will forever be storm-shy.

The storms may pass your congregation by. But other congregations will take direct hits and be devastated by them. Only God knows who will be spared and who will survive.

This guidebook is intended to prepare you for such storms. How you and your congregation respond is up to you. The critical message is Do something! Don't thumb your nose at the storm. Begin preparing now. Don't wait to see what might happen. If you respond in just a few areas, you will be better prepared than you were yesterday. But if you have the foresight to work toward a more comprehensive plan, you will be well prepared for most of the storms that are thrown at you. My hope is that readers will examine and improve every aspect of security and safety in their congregations by developing a complete plan of action.

But above all, remember this: Regardless of the frequency and intensity of those storms, God is still in charge. Many things may happen to us, regardless of the depth of our faith or our commitment to God's church. And however we choose to respond to the things of this world, God still cares for and loves us. That will never change. Grab onto that knowledge and remain secure in it. Our God reigns.

Disclaimer

The recommendations made in this book are not intended as legal advice. The contents are meant to be used as general suggestions and to stimulate discussion within congregations. Any legal questions should be directed to appropriate legal counsel. The author and publisher are not responsible for any actions taken as a result of the material contained in this book.

NOTES

Foreword

1. See *Private Security Services* (1998), a report of the Cleveland-based market-research firm, the Freedonia Group at www. freedoniagroup.com.

2. John Keegan, *War and Our World: The 1998 Reith Lectures* (London: Hutchinson, 1998).

3. "The New Terrorists," *Peace Watch* (June 1998).

Chapter One

1. "Your Church's Money," Memo 1 (Evanston, Ill.: Risk Management Department, General Council on Finance and Administration of the United Methodist Church), January 1994.

2. Fred Lawman, untitled article (Canton, Ohio). Lawman is a former Secret Service agent and now a professional security consultant. The first six suggestions are drawn from a piece he provided specifically for this book.

3. "How to Catch a Thief," *Newscope*, Aug. 29, 1997, 2. Cites Risk Management Department, General Council on Finance and Administration of the United Methodist Church. This article is the source for the first five suggestions in this list.

Chapter Three

1. Michael L. Lindvall, *The Good News from North Haven* (New York: Simon & Schuster), 1991.

2. "Arson and Church Fires in the U.S.A.," NFPA Fact Sheet, December 1997, http://www.dps.state.lu.us:80/sfm/info/church.htm.

3. *Church Threat Assessment Guide* (Washington: Department of

Treasury; Bureau of Alcohol, Tobacco and Firearms; Arsons and Explosives Division), 1996.

4. "Contractor and Service Company Risk Control," Memo 7 (Evanston, Ill.: Risk Management Department, General Council on Finance and Administration of the United Methodist Church), January 1997.

5. "Lending Your Church Facilities," *The Insurance Advisor Series,* no. 19 (Fort Wayne, Ind.: Brotherhood Mutual Insurance Co.), February 1997.

Chapter Four

1. Celia Sibley, "Abduction Puts Focus on Need for Security," *Atlanta Journal and Constitution,* May 29, 1997, JO1.

2. Sibley, "Abduction," JO1.

3. Sexual Assault Information Page, August 1998, http://www.cs. utk.edu.

4. Timothy Friend, "Sexual Abuse in the Church" (El Sobrante, Calif.: unpublished article). Friend, a private investigator and consultant, prepared the quoted material for this book.

5. Friend, "Sexual Abuse in the Church."

6. Thomas Taylor, *Seven Deadly Lawsuits: How Ministers Can Avoid Litigation and Regulation* (Nashville, Tenn.: Abingdon), 1996.

Chapter Five

1. James Cobble, "Sexual Abuse in Churches Not Limited to Clergy," cited by Mary Cagney in *Christianity Today,* Oct. 6, 1997, 90.

2. "Screening Volunteers and Paid Staff Workers with Children and Youth," Memo 2 (Evanston, Ill.: Risk Management Department, General Council on Finance and Administration of the United Methodist Church), December 1996.

Chapter Six

1. James Cobble and Richard Hammer, *Legal Training Program for Church Boards,* tape series (Fort Wayne, Ind.: Brotherhood Mutual Insurance Co. and Christian Ministry Resources), 1997.

2. Thomas Taylor, "Will Your Church Be Sued?," *Christianity Today,* Jan. 1, 1997, 42.

3. "Denominational Insurance Issues" (Evanston, Ill.: Risk Manage-

ment Department, General Council on Finance and Administration of the United Methodist Church), December 1996.

4. "Protect Your Board Members," *Insurance Advisor Series,* no. 7 (Fort Wayne, Ind.: Brotherhood Mutual Insurance Co.), May 1994.

RESOURCES

Books

Bloss, Julie. *The Church Guide to Employment Law.* Matthews, N.C.: Christian Ministry Resources, 1993.

Couser, Richard B. *Ministry and the American Legal System: A Guide for Clergy, Lay Workers and Congregations.* Minneapolis: Augsburg Fortress, 1993.

Taylor, Thomas F. *Seven Deadly Lawsuits: How Ministers Can Avoid Litigation and Regulations.* Nashville: Abingdon, 1996.

Companies

Brotherhood Mutual Insurance Co., 640 Brotherhood Way, Fort Wayne, IN 46825, 219-482-8668. Its products include a project with Christian Ministry Resources—"Reducing The Risk," a video and other material on child abuse in the church.

Christian Financial Concepts, P.O. Box 2377, Gainesville, GA 30503-2377, 770-534-1000, publishes a Bible study, *How to Manage Your Money*, by Larry Burkett.

Christian Ministry Resources, P.O. Box 1098, Matthews, NC 28106, 704-841-8066, http://www.iclonline.com. Its many helpful resources include a periodical, *Church Law and Tax Report: A Review of Legal and Tax Developments Affecting Ministers,* and a pamphlet, "Churches and Risk Management for Churches: A Self Directed Audit." (See also list of books.)

Crown Ministry, 530 Crown Oak Centre Dr., Longwood, FL 32750-
    6758, 407-331-6000, publishes a 12-week study course on
    Christian finances.
Gospel Light Publications, 2300 Knoll Dr., Ventura, CA 93003,
    800-446-7735, publishes "How to Protect Your Children's Ministry
    Program from Liability," by J. David Epstein, a manual and train-
    ing material, including many good sample forms.
NEXUS Solutions, Fort Collins, Colo., 888-639-8788, produces com-
    prehensive materials on church school and child and youth pro-
    tection in congregations, including a training manual, guidebook,
    audits, and sample forms.

Nonprofit Organizations

Christian Law Association, P.O. Box 4010, Seminole, FL 33775-4010,
    727-399-8300, provides training and legal work to churches and
    individual Christians.
Christian Legal Society, 4208 Evergreen Lane, Suite 222, Annandale,
    VA 22003, 703-642-1070, http://www.clsnet.org. CLS is a pro-
    vider of legal referrals and resources for congregational legal
    matters.